# Know Your Bible

# Know Your Bible:
# A Brief Introduction to
# the Scriptures

## Volume I
## *Analytical*
## *The Old Testament*

## Dr W. Graham Scroggie

**Authentic**

MILTON KEYNES ● COLORADO SPRINGS ● HYDERABAD

Copyright © 1940 Dr W. Graham Scroggie
First published 1940 by Pickering and Inglis, Glasgow

15 14 13 12 11 10 09  7 6 5 4 3 2 1

This edition first published 2009 by Authentic Media
and 10ofthose.com
9 Holdom Avenue, Bletchley, Milton Keynes, Bucks, MK1 1QR, UK
1820 Jet Stream Drive, Colorado Springs, CO 80921, USA
Medchal Road, Jeedimetla Village, Secunderabad 500 055, A.P., India
www.authenticmedia.co.uk

Authentic Media is a division of IBS-STL U.K., limited by guarantee,
with its  Registered Office at Kingstown Broadway, Carlisle,
Cumbria, CA3 0HA.
Registered in England & Wales No. 1216232. Registered charity
270162.

**British Library Cataloguing in Publication Data**
A catalogue record for this book is available from the British Library

ISBN 13: 978-1-85078-850-8

Cover design by Dan Collins
Print Management by Adare
Printed and bound in the UK by J.F. Print Ltd., Sparkford, Somerset

To the members of Spurgeon's Tabernacle, London, to whom it is my privilege to minister in holy things, I dedicate these volumes on 'Know Your Bible', in grateful appreciation of their love of the truth, their gracious affection, and their unfailing loyalty.

# Contents

# Foreword

This is the first of two volumes which, together, survey analytically the whole Bible. The treatment aims to be concise and helpful, and is designed to create a more widespread interest in the Scriptures.

The method in this volume, and that on the New Testament to follow, is to provide a brief introduction to each of the books of the Bible, and also to the various groups of books, together with a detailed analysis of each.

The approach throughout is practical, and not critical, and so, much is assumed which might be argued.

Questions of chronology and authorship must always be of secondary importance, and until we can speak on these subjects with more assurance than is possible at present, we shall here follow conservative views on both these subjects, without emphasis or dogmatism, and with a mind open to all new light that may be given. An event is always of more importance than the time of it, and the books, such as the epistle to the Hebrews, have a value which is independent of the question of authorship.

It is questionable whether there is any sound basis for
Scripture chronology before the time of the Monarchy,
yet we may accept a provisional scheme, such as
Bishop Ussher's, to get a general idea of the Bible
periods, while always remembering that such a scheme
is not authoritative, and in places is probably incorrect.
The values of the Bible are moral and spiritual, and
all other values are subordinate to these. The average
reader of the Scriptures has little interest, I believe, in
critical questions, important as these are for theology
students, but it is of tremendous importance that by the
Scriptures we know our God.

In the present volume the books are viewed
separately. We should remember that the divisions into
chapters and verses are altogether artificial, and that
these analyses are only a guide to thought, and to aid
memory, and were never in the minds of the writers of
these Scriptures. One of the dangers of such analytical
work is that it may prevent one apprehending and
appreciating the literary values of the books; but if we
are alive to that danger we shall not succumb to it. The
benefit of the following pages will be felt only by those
who follow the Scripture text with the outlines. For
the careful and constant reading of the text there is no
substitute.

A word must be said about the arrangement of the
books. The order in our Bibles is not chronological, but is
on a grouping plan. In the Old Testament the historical
writings are all together first, then, the poetical and
wisdom writings, and finally, the prophetical writings.
In like manner, in the New Testament, the historical
come first, then the doctrinal, and finally the prophetical.
A strictly chronological arrangement would entirely
break with this classification, and might confuse the
general reader, so I have ventured upon a compromise,

namely, chronological order within the groups. Thus, the Old Testament prophets are kept together, but are in their supposed chronological order; the gospels are kept together, but Mark comes first; and Paul's letters are kept together, but are in the order in which they were written. Of the epistles, James is believed to be the earliest, but it is kept in the Catholic group. This amended order will help us to discern how our Bible grew to its completion.

All these writings are divided into two main groups, which are called the Old and New Testaments, or covenants. These are vitally related to one another, and reveal the progress of the divine revelation. The old covenant is of law, and the new is of grace, and the one led to the other (Gal. 3:17–25). The new is in the old contained, and the old is in the new explained. The old commences what the new completes. The old gathers round Sinai, and the new round Calvary. The old is associated with Moses, and the new with Christ (Jn. 1:17). Without the new covenant the old is a start that has no finish; and without the old the new is a finish that has no start.

These covenants are related to one another as were the cherubim on the Mercy Seat, facing and answering to one another.

In the Old Testament are thirty-nine books, and in the New are twenty-seven, and these sixty-six constitute our Bible.

# Introduction

It has become fashionable with some to exalt the New Testament at the expense of the Old, and, except for its literary value in places, to regard it as having only an antiquarian interest. This, however, is as far from the truth as anything could be.

The literary value of some of these thirty-nine books is very great, but their cumulative ethical and religious value is incalculable. Here the foundations of religion are laid in the revelation of the one and only true God. Here the sin-blight in its origin and development is disclosed, the curse which separates humans from God. Here is clearly taught the utter inability of the law to bring to us the salvation we need. Here is anticipated the saving purpose and plan of God, in prophecies and types. Here the Salvation Himself is promised, the Son, the Servant, in Prophet, the Priest, and the King. Here we find men at grips with great moral problems, such as of sin, and of suffering. Here is made evident the immanence of God in history, and the fact that a principle of righteousness underlies universal government. Here all the chords of the human heart are swept in immortal songs. And here we learn of the rise and progress of that people to whom God was pleased to reveal His purpose, and by whom He is fulfilling it through Jesus Christ.

Although these books were written at different times, and by different persons, across a period of some sixteen hundred years, there is discernible progress in them, both historical and doctrinal.

Historically, there is progress from a nomadic state to national life, and from precarious leadership to the order of a kingdom. And doctrinally there is a steady movement forward from the law of Sinai to the Sermon on the Mount: from outward observance of the law of God to inward conformity to it; and from domestic and tribal to individual responsibility. The family of Genesis expands into a nation from the exodus and onwards, and contracts into a church from the exile.

The writings of the Old Testament are divisible broadly into three classes: history; literature; and legislative and genealogical material. The Bible reader will have no difficulty in differentiating these. To history belong Genesis, Exodus, Numbers, Joshua to Esther, and parts of Daniel; to literature belong Job, parts of Deuteronomy, Psalms, Proverbs, Ecclesiastes, Song of Songs, and all the prophetical books; and to the third division belong Leviticus, parts of Deuteronomy, parts of 1 Chronicles, and parts of Ezra and Nehemiah.

Through these millenniums we may trace the development of the redemptive purpose through the ante-diluvian and post-diluvian periods; the patriarchal period; the period of Egyptian enslavement and of wilderness wandering; the period of Joshua and the Judges; the period of the kingdom united, divided, and single; the period of Babylonian captivity; and the post-exilic period to the end of Old Testament history in Nehemiah. Of the remaining 400 years, until the

Messiah's advent, we have no canonical records, but most valuable history and literature are to be found in the Apocrypha.

Through all these ages 'one increasing purpose runs', a way is being prepared for the feet of the Redeemer. The revelation is organic and progressive, and it is consummated in Christ.

These writings raise endless critical questions, but such should never be allowed to obscure from our vision, nor dull our appreciation of, the ethical and spiritual value and authority of these books. They are an integral part of the 'Word of God, which liveth and abideth for ever'.

# The Pentateuchal Writings

# 1

# Introduction

The Hebrew Bible is divided into three main parts
which, in Luke 24:44, are called the Law, the Prophets,
and the Psalms, the third part being called the Psalms
because the Psalter is first in that group of books. The
Law, or Torah, comprises the first five books of the
Old Testament, as the word Pentateuch indicates. Why
there are only five books in this group we cannot say,
but it is interesting to observe that the Psalter is in five
parts, and that another group of Hebrew writings, the
'Megilloth', or Rolls, also comprises five books, Ruth,
Esther, Song of Songs, Ecclesiastes, and Lamentations.
It is regrettable that the Pentateuch has been viewed
much more from the critical than from the spiritual
standpoint. Libraries have been written on questions of
authenticity, genuineness, authors, editors, documents,
style, date, and so on, and the consideration of these
matters may easily blind one to other great facts and
values. There is a gulf between the position that Moses
had little to do with the Pentateuch, and that he wrote
the whole of it, including the account of his own death.
Criticism is allowable and is inevitable, but results
must be based on something more substantial than
hypotheses and theories.

The Mosaic authorship of these books does not exclude the employment of existing documents. Every historian has his sources and authorities. Nor does the Mosaic authorship rule out the ideas of additions and editorial care in succeeding ages (e.g. Gen. 13:7; 36:31; Exod. 16:35; Deut. 34). We may assume, therefore, that in the Pentateuch are pre-Mosaic and post-Mosaic elements, but that the dominating element is Mosaic. Here are the writings, and they constitute a unity, giving the Hebrew cosmogony, the origin of the people of Israel, and the foundation of their national constitution.

It is most probable that the Book of the Law, which was found in the Temple in the days of Josiah (2 Chron. 34) was the Pentateuch, and there is no reason to doubt that it was the Pentateuch, which Ezra read to the people in 445 BC (Neh. 8).

The historical, literary, biographical, ethical, legislative, prophetical and spiritual values of these books are beyond estimate. These are their true values, and can little be affected by purely critical considerations.

# 2

# Genesis

Keyword: election
Chapters: 50

The title *Genesis*, which is Greek, means 'origin', and the first word in the Hebrew means 'beginning', words which indicate both the scope and the limits of the book. As to scope; Genesis tells us of the beginning of everything, except God. The beginning of the universe, of life, of the human race, of the Sabbath, of covenants, of nomenclature, of marriage, of sin, of redemption, of death, of family life, of sacrifices, of nations, of government, of music, of literature, of art, of agriculture, of mechanics, of cities, and of languages; indeed, of everything that we know. As to its limits, it is only the beginning; there is here no finality. It is a kind of daybreak book, a wondrous dawn, an hour of revelation and vision. It is the seed basket out of which the harvest of all after revelation comes; it is the fountainhead from whence flows 'the river of God which is full of water'; it is the mighty root from which has spread throughout the world the Tree 'whose leaves are for the healing of the nations'; it is the small window through which may be seen, beyond the dark valley, the land of delights; it is the foundation on which the whole super-structure of divine revelation rests.

Genesis should be studied historically, prophetically, dispensationally, typically and spiritually. Its outstanding characters are Abel, Noah, Abraham, Jacob, and Joseph. Its outstanding events are the Creation, the Fall, the Deluge, the Call of Abram, and the Descent into Egypt. Its outstanding prophecy is chapter 3:15.

Divine electing grace dominates the book. Of Adam's sons, Cain drops out, and Seth is taken; of Noah's sons, Ham and Japheth drop out, and Shem is taken; of Terah's sons, Nahor and Haran drop out, and Abram is taken; of Abram's sons, Ishmael drops out, and Isaac is taken; of Isaac's sons, Esau drops out, and Jacob is taken; and of Jacob's sons, Judah is elected to be the line of the Messiah (chapter 49:10). Beneath and behind the historic redemption is the eternal election (Eph. 1:4).

## Analysis of Genesis

### I. PRIMITIVE HISTORY (1:1–11:9)

**1. From the Creation to the Fall (chs. 1–3)**
(i.)   The Creation, and God's Week of Work     1:1–2:3
(ii.)  The Garden, and the Probation of Man     2:4–25
(iii.) The Serpent, and the Fall of Eve and Adam     3

**2. From the Fall to the Flood (4:1–8:14)**
(i.)   Cain and Abel, and their Offerings     4:1–16
(ii.)  The Genealogies of Cain and Seth     4:17–5:32
(iii.) The Great Apostasy, and Divine
       Judgment     6:1–8:14

## 4. The Story of Joseph (30:22–50)

# 3

# Exodus

Keyword: redemption
Chapters: 40

The title *Exodus*, which is Greek, means 'way out', or departure, and the book tells of the deliverance of the Israelites from Egyptian bondage. From the departure, recorded in chapter 12, to the end of the book, chapter 40, is a period of about one year. The sons of Jacob have become the people Israel, a family has become a nation. First, we see them crushed, and hear them crying; next, we see them freed, led and fed; then, we see them taught and established. Chapters 1–18 are historical, and chapters 19–40 are legislative. The book should be studied geographically, biographically, and institutionally. Its outstanding character is Moses. Its outstanding events are the Training of Moses, the Ten Plagues, which were judgments against the gods of Egypt, the Institution of the Passover, the Exodus, the Giving of the Law, the Prescription of a Ritual, the Appointment of a Priesthood, and the Construction of the Tabernacle.

Following on from *election* in Genesis is *redemption* in Exodus. The need of it is seen in the people's condition and consciousness (chapters 1–2); the way of it is by blood (chapter 12), and power (chapter 14); the law of it is the divine will, set forth in the Decalogue, and the Book of the Covenant, and the medium of it is set forth in the Tabernacle and its institutions.

The connection between Genesis and Exodus is intimate. In the one God's purpose is revealed, and in the other God's performance is exhibited. In the one are human effort and failure, and in the other are divine power and triumph. In the one is a word of promise, and in the other is a work of fulfilment. In the one is a people chosen, and in the other is a people called. In the one is God's electing mercy, and in the other is God's electing manner. In the one is the revelation of nationality, and in the other is the realisation of nationality.

# Analysis of Exodus

## I. SUBJECTION
Israel in Egypt (1–12:36)

### 1. The Persecution of the People (ch. 1)
| | |
|---|---:|
| (i.)   National Expansion | 1–7 |
| (ii.)  Cruel Exaction | 8–14 |
| (iii.) Purposed Extinction | 15–22 |

### 2. The Preparation of a Saviour (2–4:28)
| | |
|---|---:|
| (i.)  Moses the Prince in Egypt | 2:1–15a |
| (ii.) Moses the Shepherd in Midian | 2:15b–4:28 |

### 3. The Plan and Progress of Redemption (4:29–12:36)
| | |
|---|---:|
| (i.)   The First Movement – Experimental | 4:29–7:13 |
| (ii.)  The Second Movement – Evidential | 7:14–10:29 |
| (iii.) The Third Movement – Executive | 11–12:36 |

## II. EMANCIPATION
Israel from Egypt to Sinai (12:37–18:27)

**1. To the Red Sea** (12:37–14:4)

**2. Through the Red Sea** (14:5–15:21)

**3. From the Red Sea** (15:22–18:27)

## III. REVELATION
Israel at Sinai (chs. 19–40)

**1. The Will of God Disclosed (chs. 19–31)**
| | |
|---|---|
| (i.) The Law | 19–24 |
| (ii.) The Tabernacle | 25–27 |
| (iii.) The Priesthood | 28–29 |
| (iv.) The Service | 30–31 |

**2. The Will of God Contemned (chs. 32–34)**
| | |
|---|---|
| (i.) The Great Transgression | 32:1–6 |
| (ii.) The Divine Displeasure | 32:7–33 |
| (iii.) The Law and the Covenant Renewed | 34 |

**3. The Will of God Fulfilled (chs. 35–40)**
| | |
|---|---|
| (i.) The Construction of the Tabernacle | 35–39:31 |
| (ii.) The Completion of the Tabernacle | 39:32–40:33 |
| (iii.) The Consecration of the Tabernacle | 40:34–38 |

# 4

# Leviticus

Keyword: communion
Chapters: 27

The title *Leviticus* is from Levi, the priestly tribe, and the book is one of ritual and not of history. It does not advance the story of Exodus but elaborates the ritual, which is there ordained. The book is ethical in character; its value is moral and spiritual. The dominating notes are oblation, mediation, separation, sanctification.

There are five main Offerings: the Burnt, the Meal, the Peace, the Sin, and the Trespass. These are enfolded in the Passover, and the Passover is unfolded in these. There are eight great Feasts; the Sabbath, Passover, Pentecost, Trumpets, Atonement, Tabernacles, the Sabbatic year, and Jubilee. Here is a Sabbatic system: seventh day, seventh week, seventh month, seventh year, and a heptade of years.

The outstanding character is Aaron and the outstanding chapter is the sixteenth, which tells of the day of atonement. It is important to observe where priesthood is introduced as an office; it is for a people already redeemed. Christ is the High Priest only of believers. As Aaron and his successors acted only on the behalf of the people of Israel, who had been behind Passover blood, so Christ is the fulfilment of that type only on the behalf of the Christian church. There is no priesthood on the behalf of the world. Mark the connection between Exodus and Leviticus. In the one the people are brought close to God, and in the other they are kept close. In the one is the fact of Atonement, and in the other is the doctrine of it. Exodus begins with sinners, but Leviticus begins with saints (that is, as to their standing, though not necessarily so as to their state). In Exodus we read of God's approach to us, but in Leviticus, of our approach to God. In the one book Christ is the saviour, and in the other He is the sanctifier. In Exodus our guilt is prominent, but in Leviticus, our defilement. Exodus reveals God as love, and Leviticus reveals Him as light. In the one, we are brought into union with Him, and in the other we are brought into communion. Exodus offers us pardon but Leviticus calls us to purity. In the one book we are delivered from Satan, and in the other we are dedicated to God. In Exodus God speaks out of the Mount, but in Leviticus He speaks out of the Tabernacle.

## Analysis of Leviticus

### I. THE WAY TO GOD BY SACRIFICE
Privilege (chs. 1–10)
The Work of the Son for us.
Judicial. Objective.
What He is and does.

### 1. Oblation. The Law of the Offerings (chs. 1–7)
(i.)   The Character of the Offerings                    1–6:7

(a) Complete Consecration. (1) Burnt Offering:
ch. 1: Perfect in Death – Godward. (2) Meal
Offering: ch. 2: Perfect in Life – Manward.
(b) Cloudless Communion. (3) Peace Offering:
ch. 3: Fellowship with the Father. Fellowship
with the Saints.
(c) Continued Cleansing. (4) Sin Offering: ch. 4:
Iniquity. Sin. Godward. (5) Trespass Offering:
ch. 5: Injury. Sins. Manward.

## 2. Mediation. The Law of the Priesthood (chs. 8–10)

## II. THE WALK WITH GOD BY SANCTIFICATION
Practice (chs. 11–25)
The Work of the Spirit in us.
Experimental. Subjective.
What we are to Become and Do.

**1. Separation. The Law of Purity (chs. 11–16)**

**2. Sanctification. The Law of Holiness (chs. 17–25)**

# 5

# Numbers

The title *Numbers*, which is from the Greek, is given to this book because of the double numbering or census of the people (chs. 1–4; 26). It gives the history of the journeyings of the Israelites from their departure from Sinai until they arrived in the Plains of Moab. The book covers a period of about thirty-eight years, and of the twenty-seven chapters (10–36), which tell of events after the people left Sinai, seventeen are occupied with the history of the last year (20–36). Chapters 15–19 represent a period of about thirty-seven years, the time of the *wanderings*, as distinguished from the *journeyings*, and here no itinerary is given. The movements of God's people out of His will are not on His calendar.

Outstanding characters in this narrative are Joshua and Caleb, the only two to enter Canaan, of the older generation which left Egypt. The outstanding chapters are the thirteenth and fourteenth, which tell of the great rebellion at Kadesh.

Between the nation's Egyptian and Babylonian captivities there were three great rebellions: this one in 1490 BC; the one in the time of Samuel, in 1095 BC, when they demanded a king; and the one in 975 BC when the kingdom broke into two after the death of Solomon.

This book is remarkable for the number of fragments of ancient poetry preserved in it, showing, incidentally, the use in the Pentateuch of other writings (cf. 6:24–26; 10:35,36; 21:14,15,17,18,27–30). Moses, Aaron, and Miriam all died before the people entered into the land; law, priesthood, and prophecy bring us to the borders of our inheritance, but only Joshua can bring us into it.

As Exodus is connected with Genesis, and Leviticus with Exodus, so is Numbers with Leviticus. In Leviticus the subject is the believer's worship, but in Numbers it is the believer's walk. The one treats purity, and the other pilgrimage. The one speaks of our spiritual position, and the other, of our spiritual progress. The one is concerned with our condition within, and the other, with our conduct without. Leviticus is ceremonial, and Numbers is historical. In the one the sanctuary is prominent, and in the other, the wilderness. The one emphasizes privileges, and the other, responsibilities. The one calls to fellowship with God, and the other, to faithfulness to God. Leviticus speaks of the priests, and access to God, and Numbers of the Levites, and service for men.

# Analysis of Numbers

## I. ARRAY. PREPARATION FOR THE JOURNEY
### (1:1–10:10)
### The encampment at Sinai

### 1. Organization of the Camp (chs. 1–4)
| | | |
|---|---|---|
| (i.) | Number of the Men of War | 1 |
| (ii.) | Order of the Camp | 2 |
| (iii.) | Separation and Number of the Levites | 3 |
| (iv.) | Service and Number of the Levites | 4 |

### 2. Purification of the People (chs. 5–6)
| | | |
|---|---|---|
| (i.) | Law of the Leper | 5:1–4 |
| (ii.) | Law of Trespass against a Fellow | 5:5–10 |
| (iii.) | Law of Husband and Wife | 5:11–31 |
| (iv.) | Law of the Nazarite | 6:1–21 |
| (v.) | The Priestly Blessing on Israel | 6:22–27 |

### 3. Provision for the Service (7–9:14)
| | | |
|---|---|---|
| (i.) | Dedication of the Altar | 7 |
| (ii.) | Consecration of the Levites | 8 |
| (iii.) | Celebration of the Passover | 9:1–14 |

### 4. Anticipation of the March (9:15–10:10)
| | | |
|---|---|---|
| (i.) | The Law of the Cloud | 9:15–23 |
| (ii.) | The Law of the Trumpets | 10:1–10 |

## II. ADVANCE. DISAFFECTION ON THE JOURNEY
### (10:11–14:45)
### From Sinai to Kadesh

### 1. The Departure from Sinai (10:11–36)

### 2. The Complaint at Taberah (11:1–3)

## 3. The Lusting at Kibroth-Hattaavah (11:4–35)

## 4. The Sedition at Hazeroth (12)

## 5. The Apostasy at Kadesh Barnea (13–14)

## III. RETREAT. INTERRUPTION OF THE JOURNEY
### (chs. 15–19)
From the first to the second visit to Kadesh

## 1. Legislation for the Future (15)

## 2. Insurrection of the Princes (16)

## 3. Vindication of the Priesthood (17)

## 4. Direction of the Priests and Levites (18)

## 5. Provision against Pollution (19)

## IV. RETURN. CONTINUATION OF THE JOURNEY
### (chs. 20–36)
From Kadesh to the Plains of Moab

## 1. The Return to Kadesh (20:1–21)

## 2. The Sojourn at Mount Hor (20:22–21:3)

**3. The March through the Arabah (21:4–9)**

**4. In the Coasts of the East (21:10–35)**

**5. The Encampment at Shittim (chs. 22–36)**

# 6

# Deuteronomy

The title *Deuteronomy*, which is from the Greek, and means 'the second law', is suggested by the statement in 17:18, that the coming king shall 'write him a copy of this law in a book'; for Deuteronomy is just the words copy and law together. It belongs to the period during which the Israelites were in the Plains of Moab.

The book stands in relation to the four preceding books much as John's Gospel does to the Synoptic Records, in that each gives the spiritual significance of the historical facts previously recounted. The dominating notes of the preceding books are all here: the *choice* of Genesis, the *deliverance* of Exodus, the *holiness* of Leviticus, and the *guidance* of Numbers.

Two of the other keywords of the book are remember and obey, the one pointing back to the wilderness, and the other pointing on to the land.

The three Feasts emphasized are Passover, Pentecost, and Tabernacles, referring to the past, the present, and the future.

The first part of Deuteronomy is historical; the second part is legislative; and the third part is prophetical. Moses, at the close of his life, looked upon a new generation, a new land, a new life, new duties, and a new leader, and so there was the need for this new revelation of the divine 'love', nowhere mentioned until now, though much illustrated. In chapters 1–4, we learn of God's love in the past; in chapters 5–26, of His love in the present; and in chapters 27–34, of His love in the future. No critical questions can lessen the moral and spiritual value of this great book, the orations of Moses in the Plains of Moab. It is a significant example of what De Quincey calls 'the literature of power', as distinct from 'the literature of knowledge'. It is probably true that Deuteronomy is the most spiritual book in the Old Testament.

# Analysis of Deuteronomy

## I. A REVIEW OF ISRAEL'S WANDERINGS AND GOD'S LONGSUFFERINGS
### (chs. 1:1–4:43)
### Preface: 1:1–5

### 1. From Horeb to Kadesh (1:6–46)

| | |
|---|---|
| (i.) The Order to Proceed | 6–8 |
| (ii.) The Appointment of Elders | 9–18 |
| (iii.) The Journey | 19 |
| (iv.) The Mission of the Spies | 20–25 |
| (v.) The Great Rebellion | 26–33 |
| (vi.) The Lord's Anger with Israel and Moses | 34–40 |
| (vii.) The Israelites Defeated by the Amorites | 41–46 |

## III. A REVELATION OF GOD'S FUTURE PURPOSES REGARDING ISRAEL (chs. 27–30)
Part A – The Far View (chs. 27–28)

## 2. Consequences of Obedience and Disobedience (ch. 28)

Part B—The Near View (chs. 29–30)

## 1. In the Wilderness (29:1–9)

## 2. In the Land (29:10–21)

## 3. In Captivity (29:22–29)

## 4. In the Land Again (30:1–10)

## 5. The Final Appeal (30:11–20)

# IV. A RECORD OF THE CLOSING EVENTS OF MOSES' LIFE
## (chs. 31–34)

## 1. Four Solemn Charges (31:1–29)

## 2. The Prophetic Song of Moses (31:30–32:47)

## 3. The Final Events (32:48–34:12)

# The Historical Writings

# 7

# Introduction

This classification is general, and for the sake of convenience, and it must be remembered that large parts of the Pentateuch, and parts of the later prophetical books are also historical.

The period covered by these books reaches from the death of Moses in 1451 BC, to the end of Old Testament history, about 396 BC, that is, approximately 1055 years, a long time in the history of a people.

This long period falls into three main parts, namely, first, from the death of Moses to the accession of Saul, 1451–1096 BC, that is 355 years: second, from the accession of Saul to the overthrow of Judah, 1096–586 BC, that is 510 years: and third, from the overthrow of Judah to the end of Old Testament history, 586–396 BC, that is 190 years. By getting that perspective it will be easier to follow the unfolding story. These periods represent three forms of government, relative to the chosen nation, first, the Theocracy, or rule of God; second, the Monarchy, or rule of kings of their own; and third, the Dependency, or rule of alien kings.

It must be remembered that the Old Testament story is history with a religious purpose, and selection and omission are determined by this fact. That millennium was the period of great civilisations, great characters, great cities, and great conflicts of Babylonia, Egypt, Assyria, Phoenicia, Syria, Greece, and Persia; yet, all this fascinating story has no place in the Bible record except in so far as these powers and persons came into contact with this chosen people. And not only so, but in the history of Israel itself, much is passed over briefly which we would consider of great historical importance, while events of seeming minor importance are recorded at length. The reason for this is that the purpose of Old Testament history is moral and spiritual, and not annalistic; it is the history of God's self-revelation for the redemption of men. All omissions and digressions must be received in this light.

Herodotus is commonly regarded as the father of history, but the Hebrews wrote history a thousand years before Herodotus was born.

That in these writings other documents are named, as the depositories of ampler information, and that some of the books were written or collected long after the event they describe, are facts which create no difficulty, and are in accordance with what we know of the general method of revelation. They account, moreover, for the occasional blending of matter evidently contemporaneous with the events described with others of clearly later origin.

Although these books were written by different persons, at different times, and in different places, they yet present a coherent and constructive account of a thousand years of history. This can be accounted for only by assuming a divine providence and inspiration.

The dates attached to the following books are given without dogmatism.

# 8

# Joshua

Keyword: possession
Chapters: 24
Date: 1451–1426 BC
25 years

This book bears the name of Joshua because he is the hero of it, although, no doubt, Jewish tradition is right in assuming that he also supplied the materials of the story, which were supplemented and edited by some later scribes. This book goes on from where Deuteronomy leaves off; Joshua completes what Moses commenced. The great event in Moses' life was the passage through the Red Sea, and the great event in Joshua's life was the passage through the Jordan. The one tells of deliverance from bondage, and the other of entrance into blessing. Moses' symbol was the rod, but Joshua's was the spear. The connection between Deuteronomy and Joshua is instructive. In the one is a prospect, but in the other, an experience. In the one is the vision of faith, and in the other, the venture of faith. In the one is Israel's inheritance, and in the other,

Israel's possession. In the one is the call to conflict, and in the other is the clash of conflict.

In the one is faith in principle, and in the other, faith in action. In the one is the ideal to become actual, and in the other the ideal becomes actual. In the one is possibility, and in the other realisation. The New Testament counterparts of this book are the Acts and Ephesians.

# Analysis of Joshua

## I. ENTERING THE LAND (1:1–5:12)

### 1. Preparation of the People (1:1–3:13)

### 2. Passage of the People (3:14–4:24)

### 3. Purification of the People (5:1–12)

## II. CONQUERING THE LAND (5:13–12:24)

### 1. The Revelation of Victory (5:13–15)

### 2. The Realization of Victory (chs. 6–11)

### 3. The Record of Victory (ch. 12)

## III. POSSESSING THE LAND (chs. 13–24)

### 1. Distribution of the Land among the Tribes (chs. 13–21)

### 2. Dispute about an Altar on the Border (ch. 22)

### 3. Discourse and Death of Joshua (chs. 23–24)

# 9

# Judges

Keyword: declension
Chapters: 21
Date: 1426–1096 BC
330 years

This book takes its name from a characteristic of the period between the death of Joshua and the accession of Saul, namely, the rule of *Judges*, or saviours, whom God raised up to deliver His oppressed people. Of these there were fifteen, Othniel, Ehuid, Shamgar, Deborah-Barak, Gideon, Abimelech, Tola, Jair, Jephthah, Ibzan, Elon, Abdon, Samson, Eli, and Samuel. There were three leading types, the Warrior-Judge, as Gideon and Samson; the Priest-Judge, as Eli; and the Prophet-Judge, as Samuel. The chief of these Judges were Deborah, Gideon, Samson, and Samuel.

The period of the Judges cannot be determined with any precision; calculations have a varying margin of more than a century. We cannot conclude that all these Judgeships were consecutive; indeed, it is almost certain that some of them were contemporaneous; but we may reckon about 330 years for this period.

Nothing is known as to the authorship of the book, though tradition ascribes it to Samuel. Clearly it is a compilation, and may not have taken its present form until several centuries after the events it records.

The main narrative is in 3:7–16:31, and 1 Sam. 1–7; and chapters 17–25, with Ruth, are undated episodes of the early days of the Judges, inserted between the histories of Samson and Samuel.

Judges is one of the saddest books in the Bible, telling, as it does, of repeated apostasy, chastisement, and mercy. Rebellion, retribution, repentance, and rest, are the dominating notes in this minor music. Joshua treats of the heavenlies, but Judges of the earthlies; the one is of the Spirit, and the other is of the flesh. In the one is a song of joy, and in the other a sob of sorrow. In the one is victory, and in the other, defeat. In the one is progress, and in the other, decline: in the one, faith, and in the other, unbelief: in the one freedom, and in the other bondage. Judges teaches us, on the one hand, not to presume, and on the other hand, not to despair.

# 10

# Ruth

Keyword: restoration
Chapters: 4

This is one of the only two books of the Bible which bear the name of a woman, and in many respects they present remarkable contrasts. The one is of a Gentile woman, Ruth, who was brought into the midst of Jews, among whom she henceforth lives her life; and the other is of a Jewish woman, Esther, who is taken into the midst of Gentiles, where, with equal fidelity and grace, she plays the part ordained for her by God. Ruth is a lovely pastoral idyll, the tale of a friendship between two women, and the grand climax is the birth of a baby. After reading Judges 17–21, Ruth is like a beautiful lily in a stagnant pool. Here, instead of unfaithfulness, is loyalty, and instead of immorality, is purity. Here, instead of battlefields are harvest fields, and instead of the warrior's shout is the harvester's song.

Ruth's protestation of love for Naomi is as eloquent a passage as can be found in the whole range of world literature (Ruth 1:16,17).

The story has a typical significance, which may be discerned in the meanings of the names which occur:

Bethlehem, House of Bread;
Elimelech, My God is King;
Naomi, Sweet (?);
Mahlon, Song;
Chilion, Perfection;
Ruth, Satisfied;
Orpah, skull (?);
Boaz, Strength.

These three women represent: a saint backsliding, Naomi; a sinner rejecting blessing, Orpah; and a sinner believing and blessed, Ruth. Boaz may be regarded as a type of Christ, as lord of harvest (2:3), dispenser of bread (3:15), kinsman-redeemer (2:20), giver of rest (3:1), man of wealth (2:1), and our strength.

This book is one of the Megilloth or Festal Rolls, one of which was publicly read at each festival, Ruth being read at the feast of Pentecost. One of the designs of the book is to trace the descent of David, and to show that the Gentiles are not outside the scope of redeeming love.

The analysis of Ruth and Judges are combined.

# Analysis of Judges and Ruth

## I. INTRODUCTION (1–3:6)

### 1. Retrospective (1:1–2:10)

**2. Prospective (2:11–3:6)**
(i.) A Summary of the Period        2:11–23
     (a) Rebellion
     (b) Retribution
     (c) Repentance
     (d) Rest
(ii.) A Summary of the Enemies        3:1–6

## II. THE HISTORY (3:7–16:31)

**1. First Cycle (3:7–11)**

| | |
|---|---|
| Enemy | *Mesopotamia* |
| Subjection | 8 years |
| Deliverer | *Othniel* |
| Peace | 40 years |

**2. Second Cycle (3:12–31)**

| | |
|---|---|
| Enemy | *Moabites, Ammonites, Amalekites* |
| Subjection | 18 years |
| Deliverer | *Ehud* |
| Peace | 80 years |

(3:31–Shamgar delivers from the Philistines.)

**3. Third Cycle (4:1–5:31)**

| | |
|---|---|
| Enemy | *Canaanites* |
| Subjection | 20 years |
| Deliverer | *Deborah* and *Barak* |
| Peace | 40 years |

**4. Fourth Cycle (6:1–8:32)**

| | |
|---|---|
| Enemy | *Midianites* |
| Subjection | 7 years |
| Deliverer | *Gideon* |
| Peace | 40 years |

## 5. Fifth Cycle (8:33–10:5)

| | |
|---|---:|
| Usurpation of *Abimelech* | 3 years |
| Judgeship of *Tola* and *Jair* | 45 years |

## 6. Sixth Cycle (10:6–12:15)

| | |
|---|---|
| Enemy | *Ammonites* |
| Subjection | 18 years |
| Deliverer | *Jephthah* |
| Peace | 31 years |

## 7. Seventh Cycle (chs. 13–16)

| | |
|---|---|
| Enemy | *Philistines* |
| Subjection | 40 years |
| Deliverer | *Samson* |
| Peace | 20 years |

## III. APPENDIX (chs. 17–21, Ruth)

### 1. Micah and the Danites (chs. 17–18)
*Infidelity*

### 2. A Levite's Concubine (chs. 19–20)
*Immorality*

### 3. The Story of Ruth
*Fidelity and Morality*

# 11

# 1 Samuel

Keyword: kingdom
Chapters: 31
Date: 1150 (?) –1055 BC
95 years

In this record ends what Professor R. Moulton calls 'incidental history', and commences what he calls 'regular history'. The long period of the Judges, with its unsettled government, terminates with the judgeship of Samuel, and five centuries of Monarchy start (1095–586 BC). The book may be divided into three unequal parts by a grouping of its chief characters, Eli, Samuel, Saul, and David, but it should be discerned that these parts overlap. In all likelihood chapters 1–24 were written by Samuel, and 25–31 by Nathan and Gad (10:25; 1 Chron. 29:29).

The Warrior-Judges have passed, and a Priest-Judge has come, Eli, to be followed by a Prophet-Judge, Samuel, and with him the period of the Judges ends, and the Order of the Prophets begins (Acts 13:20; 3:24). Until now the priest had been prominent, and from now the prophet is distinguished. By the former, the people drew close to God, and by the latter God drew close to the people. Christ is both Prophet and Priest, the former, when here on earth, and the latter, now in heaven. This book is rich in character studies.

Eli was probably contemporary with Samson, and he ministered from the Sanctuary in Shiloh for forty years. When Samuel was born Eli was physically old and spiritually weak, and his sons 'were sons of Belial; they knew not the Lord' (1 Sam. 2:12).

Samuel is one of the greatest of the Hebrew worthies, whose influence lay not in military exploits, nor in diplomatic skill, nor in political shrewdness, but in unswerving integrity and splendid loyalty to God (12:1–3). He is the third of the great leaders whom God raised up for Israel (Abraham, Moses, Samuel) and he is the first of three great transition-period leaders. He saw the outgoing of the Theocracy and the incoming of the Monarchy. Jeremiah saw the outgoing of the Monarchy and the incoming of the Dependency, and Paul saw the outgoing of Judaism and the incoming of Christianity.

Saul is a strange character, exciting in us both admiration and pity; a man whom Samuel sternly rebuked (15:20–23), and whom David lavishly praised (2 Sam. 1:19–27); a man whose morning was bright, but soon became overcast, and whose sun set in blackest clouds. Follow carefully his rise, his reign, and his ruin. It's helpful to read Browning's 'Saul'.

David is one of the greatest characters of all time, having regard to his influence upon history, national and spiritual. In this book we see him as shepherd lad, minstrel, armour-bearer, captain, king's son-in-law, king designate, psalmist, and fugitive. He was thrice anointed, and was the founder of the royal line of which the King of kings came.

Jonathan is a choice soul, the two chief features of whose story are, his self-suppression, and his love for David (1 Sam. 18, 20; 2 Sam. 1:26). Other noteworthy features of this book are the founding of prophetic schools, the commencement of the Monarchy, the defeat of the Philistines by the slaying of Goliath, the Song of Hannah, the first occurrence of 'Messiah' (chapter 2:10 Heb.), the campaigns against the Ammonites, Amalekites, and Philistines, and the battle at Mount Gilboa, with which the historical part of Chronicles begins (chapter 10).

# Analysis of 1 Samuel

## I. ELI AND SAMUEL (chs. 1–7)

### 1. Contrasted Family Life in Shiloh (chs. 1–3)

(i.)  Elkanah and his son. Righteous.

| | |
|---|---|
| (a) The Birth of Samuel | (1:1–2:11) |
| (b) The Ministry of Samuel | (2:18–21,26) |
| (c) The Call of Samuel | (3:1–21) |

(ii.)  Eli and his sons. Wicked.

| | |
|---|---|
| (a) Their Sin | (2:12–17,22–25) |
| (b) Their Sentence | (2:27–36) |

### 2. The Philistines and the Ark of God (chs. 4–7)

(i.)  The Philistines Victorious  —  4–7:1

| | |
|---|---|
| (a) The Ark Taken | (4) |
| (b) The Ark Held | (5) |
| (c) The Ark Returned | (6:1–7:1) |

(ii.)  The Philistines Defeated  —  7:2–17

| | |
|---|---|
| (a) The Dedication at Mizpeh | (2–6) |
| (b) The Victory of Israel | (7–12) |
| (c) The Judgeship of Samuel | (13–17) |

## II. SAMUEL AND SAUL (chs. 8–15)

## III. SAUL AND DAVID (chs. 16–31)

# 12

# 2 Samuel

Keyword: consolidation
Chapters: 24
Date: 1055–1015 BC
40 years
Parallel history: 1 Chronicles 11–29

This is an account of greatest importance, and of thrilling interest. In these historical books, 1–2 Samuel, 1–2 Kings, a dramatic development is discernible; Samuel supersedes Eli, Saul supersedes Samuel, David supersedes Saul, and David's sons supersede their father. The Hebrew Monarchy proper began with David, and in his reign it reached its highest development. He unified the nation, obtained for it a royal capital, subdued its enemies, and extended the kingdom from the Red Sea to the river Orontes, and from the Mediterranean to the Euphrates. He created a national consciousness, and brought prosperity by extending trade. It has been well said that 'four streams of influence have come to us from his times. First, by establishing the City of David he set in motion all that Jerusalem has meant in war and in song. Secondly, he founded a dynasty, and the sanctity, the authority, the splendour of the House of David have moulded the hopes of Israel and the forms of Christian faith through all subsequent generations. Thirdly, his reign was marked by a signal development of poetry and music; he is credited with the orchestration of wind, stringed, and percussion instruments; and with nobler music the psalms of worship became more numerous and significant. Fourthly, about this time public records were kept with systematic care. Samuel left written documents (1 Sam. 10:25), David appointed court recorders and scribes, Nathan the prophet wrote history (1 Chron. 29:29). Under David the harassed tribes became a conquering, self-conscious nation, and music, song, history, and prophetic dreams sprang to life' (C.A. Dinsmore).

The narrative is full of graphic and convincing detail, and is written in the best style of classical Hebrew. It begins with one of the most perfect elegies in any language, David's lament over Saul called 'The Song of the Bow', and let us remember it was written over three thousand years ago, by a young man just turned thirty.

In the Hebrew Bible First and Second Samuel are one book, as are First and Second Kings; and, indeed, the four tell one story, the story of the Monarchy from its rise to its fall. David's history begins in 1 Samuel and ends in 1 Kings and is divisible into four parts: his education (1 Sam. 16–31); his election (2 Sam. 1–10); his ejection (2 Sam. 11–18); and his exaltation (2 Sam. 19–1 Kings 2:11); or, his testings, triumphs, troubles, and testimonies. David came to the throne, conquered from the throne, fled from the throne, and was established on the throne, stages which tell of preparation, subjugation, retribution, and restoration. As a king, David's home policy was the centralisation of power and worship, in which he succeeded by taking Jerusalem and bringing the Ark to it; and his Foreign Policy was the subjugation of all enemies, and in this also he succeeded (ch. 8). Solemn indeed is the story of his fall and its consequences, whereby he has made 'the enemies of the Lord to blaspheme' for three thousand years. But profound was his repentance, and out of it came Psalms 32 and 51. The great shepherd became a great soldier, and the great sinner became a great saint.

# Analysis of 2 Samuel

## I. DAVID, KING OVER JUDAH, IN HEBRON
7 years. chs. 1–4

### 1. David and the Dead (ch. 1)
| | | |
|---|---|---|
| (i.) | A False Account of Saul's Death | 1:1–16 |
| (ii.) | David's Lamentation for Saul and Jonathan | 1:17–27 |

### 2. Two Kings Crowned (2:1–11)
| | | |
|---|---|---|
| (i.) | David over Judah | 2:1–7 |
| (ii.) | Ish-bosheth over Israel | 2:8–11 |

### 3. War Between Judah and Israel (2:12–4:12)
| | | |
|---|---|---|
| (i.) | Joab and Abner | 2:12–32 |
| (ii.) | Abner and David | 3:1–21 |
| (iii.) | Joab, David and Abner | 3:22–39 |
| (iv.) | Ish-bosheth and his Murderers | 4:1–12 |

# II. DAVID, KING OVER ALL ISRAEL, IN JERUSALEM
33 years. 2 Sam. 5–2 Kings 2:11

# 13

# 1 Kings 1–11

Keyword: glory
Chapters: 11
Date: 1015–975 BC
40 years
Parallel history: 2 Chronicles 1–9

The United Kingdom lasted for one hundred and twenty years, having three kings who each reigned for forty years (1095–975 BC). Of these, the first was of the tribe of Benjamin, and the other two of the tribe of Judah, so that the predicted Messianic line began with David (Gen. 46:10). The record of his closing days is in 1 Kings 1–2:11, where we read of Adonijah's attempt to seize the throne, of the coronation of Solomon, and of David's charge to his son and successor.

Then follows the record of Solomon's reign (1015–975 BC), in chapters 2–11, and 2 Chronicles 1–9. These few chapters contain events of great historical and spiritual significance.

Solomon was a strange character, and he may be regarded in various ways, personally, officially, and typically. Viewed personally, he was characterised by wisdom and wickedness: greatly gifted intellectually, he was very weak ethically. His mind and his morals were not on the same level. Viewed officially, his great work was twofold, the material development of the kingdom, and the erection of the Temple. The Solomonic Temple was one of the most magnificent structures of the ancient world, and it has been computed that the value of the materials used in the building of it would not be less than £100m. Viewed typically, it is not difficult to see an anticipation of Christ's Millennial Kingdom, when, after the extirpation of all His foes, there will be peace. Psalm 62, which is attributed to Solomon, reflects this view. Solomon's wisdom, and work, and waywardness unite to make him an outstanding character, whose reign and his father's constitute the golden period of the Jewish state.

# Analysis of 1 Kings 1–11 and 2 Chron. 1–9

## I. APPOINTMENT OF SOLOMON TO THE THRONE (1–2:9)

| | | |
|---|---|---|
| **1.** | Usurpation of Adonijah | 1:1–31 |
| **2.** | Ordination of Solomon | 1:32–53 |
| **3.** | Instruction of Solomon | 2:1–9 |

## II. ESTABLISHMENT OF SOLOMON ON THE THRONE (2:10–46)

| | | |
|---|---|---|
| **4.** | Execution of his Foes | 10–46 |

## III. THE WISDOM AND WEALTH
## OF SOLOMON (chs. 3–4)

## IV. THE TEMPLE AND HOUSE
## OF SOLOMON (chs. 5–10)

## V. THE SIN AND FALL
## OF SOLOMON (ch. 11)

# 14

# 1 Kings 12–2 Kings 18:12

Keyword: disruption
Chapters: 28
Date: 975–721 BC
254 years
Parallel history: 2 Chronicles 10–28

The United Kingdom record ends at 1 Kings 11, with the death of Solomon, and the Divided Kingdom record is in 1 Kings 12:1–2 Kings 18:12, together with the parallel chapters in 2 Chronicles. This part of the history of the Monarchy should be kept distinct from what preceded and what follows it, that is, from the United Kingdom on the one hand, and the Single Kingdom on the other hand. The story covers over two and a half centuries, during which time the kingdom was divided into two parts, which are spoken of as Judah, the Southern Kingdom, with its capital at Jerusalem; and Israel, the Northern Kingdom, with its capital, first at Shechem, and then at Samaria. The tribes of Judah, Benjamin, and Levi remained loyal to the Davidic House, and the others seceded, and established a new kingdom, a new centre and object of worship, a new order of priests, a new altar of sacrifice, and a new festal month.

The way in which this part of the history is arranged makes analysis difficult, so I have felt it best to tabulate the seven salient facts: the name of each king, when he began to reign, the length of his reign, the kingdom to which he belonged, his character, and the parallel references, relating also to the history and the prophets of the period. In this way the alternating records are given with distinctiveness.

The division of the kingdom, which was predicted (1 Kings 11:26–40), was due to the idolatrous disloyalty of the nation, and for this sin both parts of the kingdom were sent ultimately into captivity; Israel to Assyria, in 721 BC; and Judah to Babylonia, in 586 BC.

During the two and a half centuries of their parallel history, three periods are to be distinguished by the relation of the kingdoms to one another. From Rehoboam to Asa in the South, and from Jeroboam to Omri in the North, a period of fifty-seven years (975–918 BC, 1 Kings 12:1–16:28), they were antagonistic to one another. Then, by the marriage of Jehoshaphat's son (South) with Ahab's daughter (North), the kingdoms were allied to one another for seventy-nine years (918–839 BC; 1 Kings 16:29–2 Kings 13:9). And, finally, from Amaziah to Hezekiah in the south, and from Joash to Hoshea in the North, a period of one hundred and eighteen years, they were again antagonistic to one another (839–721 BC; 2 Kings 13:10–18:12).

When reading the record of this history certain facts should be borne in mind. In the Southern Kingdom there was but one dynasty, the Davidic, but in the Northern Kingdom there were nine dynasties. In the South were nineteen kings and one queen; in the North were nineteen kings. In the South some of the rulers were good, some unstable, and some bad; but in the North, all were bad. In the South were three religious revivals, in the reigns of Jehoshaphat, Hezekiah, and Josiah; but in the North there were no revivals. The tribes in the South were taken into Babylonian captivity by Nebuchadnezzar; and the tribes in the North, into Assyrian captivity by Shalmaneser.

The foreign powers that came into touch with the South or the North in this period were Assyria, Egypt, Babylonia, and Syria.

The best kings of Judah were Asa, Jehoshaphat, Hezekiah, and Josiah, and the worst were Ahaz and Manasseh. It should be observed that each of the best kings made a serious mistake; Asa, by his alliance with Syria against Israel; Jehoshaphat by his alliance with the House of Ahab; Hezekiah, by his friendliness to the Babylonian messengers from Merodach-Baladan; and Josiah, by his march against Pharaoh Necho, of Egypt.

This Divided Kingdom period was distinguished by prophetic ministry; oral, by Elijah and Elisha, and by minor prophets, Ahijah, Iddo, Shemiah, Jehu, Hanani, Azariah, Jahaziel, and Eliezer: and oral or (and) written ministry by Joel, Jonah, Amos, Hosea, Isaiah and Micah. It was distinguished also by miracles, of which there were seven in the days of Elijah, and eleven in the days of Elisha.

The Northern Kingdom did not advance the Messianic purpose, but the Southern Kingdom did. The Davidic succession was maintained, and by the prophets, a true witness was kept alive. Jehovah was patient with His people, albeit He visited them in judgment for their sins.

## Analysis of 1 Kings 12 – 2 Kings 18:12 and 2 Chron. 10 – 18

| King | Date | Years | Kingdom | Character | Record |
|------|------|-------|---------|-----------|--------|
| **Rehoboam and Jeroboam (1 Kings 12:1–19; 2 Chron. 10)** | | | | | |
| Rehoboam | 975 | 17 | South | Bad | 1 Kgs. 12:20–24; 14:21–31; 2 Chron. 11–2 |
| Jeroboam | 975 | 21 | North | Bad | 1 Kgs. 12:25–14:20 |
| Abijam | 958 | 2 | South | Bad | 1 Kgs. 15:1–8; 2 Chron. 13–14:1a |
| Asa | 956 | 40 | South | Good | 1 Kgs. 15:9–24; 2 Chron. 14:1b–16 |
| Nadab | 954 | 1 | North | Bad | 1 Kgs. 15:25–31 |
| Baasha | 953 | 23 | North | Bad | 1 Kgs. 15:32–16:7 |
| Elah | 930 | 1 | North | Bad | 1 Kgs. 16:8–10a |
| Zimri | 929 | 7 days | North | Bad | 1 Kgs. 16:10b–20 |
| Omri | 929 | 12 | North | Bad | 1 Kgs. 16:21–28 |
| Ahab | 917 | 12 | North | Bad | 1 Kgs. 16:29–22:40 |
| **Ministry of Elijah (1 Kings 17 – 2 Kings 2)** | | | | | |
| Jehoshaphat | 916 | 24 | South | Good | 1 Kgs. 22:2–33, 41–50; 2 Chron. 17–21:3 |
| Ahaziah | 897 | 1 | North | Bad | 1 Kgs. 22:51–2 Kg. 2:25 |

*continued over*

**Ministry of Elisha (2 Kings 2 – 13)**

| | | | |
|---|---|---|---|
| Joram | 896 | 12 | North | Bad | 2 Kgs. 3 – 8:15 |
| Jehoroam | 892 | 7 | South | Bad | 2 Kgs. 8:16 – 24; 2 Chron. 21:4 – 20 |
| Ahaziah | 885 | 1 | South | Bad | 2 Kgs. 8:25 – 29; 2 Chron. 22:1 – 9 |
| Jehu | 884 | 28 | North | Bad | 2 Kgs. 9 – 10:36 |
| Athaliah | 884 | 6 | South | Bad | 2 Kgs. 11; 2 Chron. 12:10 – 13 |
| Jehoash | 878 | 40 | South | Good | 2 Kgs. 12; 2 Chron. 24 |

**Ministry of Joel (2 Kings 12 – 17:7; 2 Chron. 24 – 26)**

| | | | |
|---|---|---|---|
| Jehoahaz | 856 | 17 | North | Bad | 2 Kgs. 13:1 – 9 |
| Joash | 839 | 16 | North | Bad | 2 Kgs. 13:10 – 25 |

**Ministry of Jonah (2 Kings 13, 14)**

| | | | |
|---|---|---|---|
| Amaziah | 838 | 29 | South | Good | 2 Kgs. 14:1 – 20; 2 Chron. 25 |
| Jeroboam II | 823 | 41 | North | Bad | 2 Kgs. 14:23 – 29 |
| | | | Interregnum of 11 – 12 years |

*continued over*

| King | Date | Years | Kingdom | Character | Record |
|---|---|---|---|---|---|
| **Ministry of Amos (2 Kings 14:21 – 15:7)** | | | | | |
| Azariah | 809 | 52 | South | Good | 2 Kgs. 14:21,22; 15:1 – 7; 2 Chron. 26 |
| Zachariah | 772 | 1/2 | North | Bad | 2 Kgs. 15:8 – 12 |
| Shallum | 772 | 1/2 | North | Bad | 2 Kgs. 15:13 – 16 |
| Menahem | 772 | 10 | North | Bad | 2 Kgs. 15:17 – 22 |
| **Ministry of Hosea (2 Kings 14:23 – 23:17)** | | | | | |
| Pekahiah | 762 | 2 | North | Bad | 2 Kgs. 15:23 – 26 |
| Pekah | 760 | 20 | North | Bad | 2 Kgs. 15:27 – 31 |
| Jotham | 757 | 15 | South | Good | 2 Kgs. 15:32 – 38; 2 Chron. 27 |
| **Ministry of Isaiah (2 Kings 15 – 20; 2 Chron. 26 – 32)** | | | | | |
| Ahaz | 742 | 16 | South | Bad | 2 Kgs. 16; 2 Chron. 28; Isa. 7 – 12 |
| | | | Interregnum of about 9 years | | |
| Hoshea | 730 | 9 | North | Bad | 2 Kgs. 17 |
| **Ministry of Micah (2 Kings 15:32 – 20; 2 Chron. 27 – 32)** | | | | | |

# 15

# 2 Kings 18–25

Keyword: downfall
Chapters: 8
Date: 721–586 BC
135 years
Parallel history: 2 Chronicles 29:1–36:21

This important period of the Monarchy's history falls into two unequal parts. First, from Judah's first reformation, under Hezekiah, to the close of Amon's reign; 721–640 BC, eighty-one years: and second, from Judah's final reformation, under Josiah, in the overthrow of the kingdom and end of the Monarchy; 640–586 BC, fifty-four years. That is to say, after the people of Israel had been removed to Assyria, the kingdom of Judah continued for one hundred and thirty-five years, during which time two great efforts were made to turn the people from idolatry. These efforts seemed for a while to be successful, but repentance was not deep, and so, in spite of the ministry of the prophets, the kingdom ran on to its fate.

Hezekiah, who reigned for twenty-nine years, is more unreservedly commended than any other king of

Judah, and the history and literature of his reign occupy 77 chapters of the Bible. It was his lot to be placed between a wicked father and a wicked son. The three great events of his reign were: Judah's deliverance from the Assyrian invasion; his own sickness and recovery; and the religious reformation which he led.

His son, Manasseh, and grandson, Amon, were both bad; the former reigned longer than any other king. Fifty-seven years after Hezekiah's death his great-grandson, Josiah, made another and final effort to bring the nation back to God, but in vain. The outstanding event in his reign was the discovery in the Temple of the Book of the Law, and the transient revival in this reign was the result of that discovery.

Isaiah was the great prophet in Hezekiah's time, and Jeremiah, the great prophet from Josiah's time. Other prophets of the Single Kingdom period were Micah, Nahum, Zephaniah, and Habakkuk.

The great foreign figures of this period were Shalmaneser, Sennacherib, Merodach-Baladan, Esarhaddon, Pharaoh-Necho, and Nebuchadnezzar – records of whom are to be found in the British Museum.

The outstanding battle was at Carchemish in 605 BC, in which the Babylonians conquered the Egyptians.

The Monarchy and the Dependency periods overlap for twenty years (606–586 BC), that is to say, though the last three kings were Jews, they had their throne by the will of foreign powers, first Egypt, and then Babylon. And it is important to see that in this score of years three prophesied events commenced: the servitude, 70 years, 606–536 BC (Jer. 29:10); the exile, 50 years, 586–536 BC; and the desolation, 70 years, 586–516 BC (Jer. 25:1–11). Twenty years of what is commonly regarded as the captivity were, in fact, not in the period of the exile, but of the servitude.

It was when Nebuchadnezzar first attacked Jerusalem, in the reign of Jehoiakim, 606 BC, that Daniel and the other three Hebrews were removed to Babylon; and when he made the second attack, in the reign of Jehoaichin (598 BC), Ezekiel and Mordecai were taken.

## Analysis of 2 Kings 18–25

| King | Date | Years | Kingdom | Character | Record |
|------|------|-------|---------|-----------|--------|
| Hezekiah | 726 | 29 | South | Good | 2 Kgs. 18–20; 2 Chron. 29–32; Isa. 36–39 |
| Manasseh | 697 | 55 | South | Bad | 2 Kgs. 21:1–18; 2 Chron. 33:1–20 |
| **Ministry of Nahum** (2 Kings 21–24:7; 2 Chron. 33–36:8) | | | | | |
| Amon | 642 | 2 | South | Bad | 2 Kgs. 21:19–26; 2 Chron. 33:21–25 |
| Josiah | 640 | 31 | South | Good | 2 Kgs. 22–23:30; 2 Chron. 34–35 |
| **Ministry of Zephaniah** (2 Kings 22–24:7; 2 Chron. 34–36:8) | | | | | |

*continued over*

## Ministry of Jeremiah
### (2 Kings 22–25; 2 Chron. 34–36:21)

| Jehoahaz | 609 | ¼ | South | Bad | 2 Kgs. 23:31–34; 2 Chron. 36:1–4 |
| Jehoiakim | 609 | 11 | South | Bad | 2 Kgs. 32:35–34:7; 2 Chron. 36:5–8 |

## Ministry of Habakkuk
### (2 Kings 23:31–24:16; 2 Chron. 36:1–10)

## Ministry of Daniel
### (2 Kings 23:35–25:30; 2 Chron. 36:5–23)

| Jehoiachin | 598 | ¼ | South | Bad | 2 Kgs. 24:8–16; 2 Chron. 36:9,10 |
| Zedekiah | 598 | 11 | South | Bad | 2 Kgs. 24:17–25:21. |
| | | | | | 2 Chron. 36:11–21; Jer. 52:1–30 |

*continued over*

**Ministry of Ezekiel**
(2 Kings 24:17 – 25:30; 2 Chron. 36:11, 572 BC)

**Ministry of Obadiah (586 BC)**
The Lamentations over the Ruins of Jerusalem.
2 Kings 25:22 – 26; 2 Chron. 36:17 – 21.
Governorship of Gedaliah. 2 Kings 25:22 – 26.
Restoration of Jehoiachin. 2 Kings 25:27 – 30; Jer. 52:31 – 34.

# 16

# 1–2 Chronicles

Keyword: worship
Chapters: 65

Unless the viewpoint of these two books is understood, there can be no true appreciation of them. Like the books of Samuel and Kings, they were originally one book, and they appear at the end of the Hebrew Bible, in the third division which is known as the Psalms. The Hebrew title is 'Word of days', that is, journals; the Septuagint title is Omissions, because they were regarded as supplementing what had already been written; and the present title, *Chronicles*, dates from the time of Jerome (4th cent. AD), and this last is, perhaps, the best description of these records.

That these writings are a compilation must be evident to the most superficial reader; nor are we left in ignorance of the sources, for no fewer than twelve are named in the text. (See 1 Chron. 9:1; 29:29; 2 Chron. 9:29; 12:15; 20:34; 24:27; 26:22; 32:32; 33:19.)

This fact does not permit of our thinking of an author, but only of a compiler of the Chronicles. The material was collected and selected with a specific end in view, and it appears to have been done with great care. Not without good reason the compiler of these records is supposed to be Ezra (cf. 2 Chron. 36:22,23, with Ezra 1:1–2). The scope of the record is noteworthy. It begins with Adam (1 Chron. 1:1) and ends with the Decree of Cyrus in 586 BC; that is, it embraces the whole sweep of Bible history in an epitomized form, and represents a period of not less than 3500 years. This fact alone gives uniqueness to the Chronicles, and invests them with peculiar interest. Considering, then, the title, the form, the compiler, and the scope of these books, we must enquire as to their object. This can be determined only by a careful comparison of them with the other historical books representing the same period. By such a comparison with the books of Samuel and Kings, we observe that in the Chronicles there are (a) identical passages, (b) omissions, and (c) additions; and when we look for an explanation of these, we find it in the essentially Levitical character of the writing. Parallels, omissions, and additions are all done to demonstrate a design, and that is to show the theocratic character of the nation's calling, to show that only as God is reverenced and obeyed can the nation prosper and fulfil her high destiny.

For this reason, after the genealogies, which give the sacred line through which the Messianic promise was transmitted for over three and a half millenniums, the annals of Judah only are given, from the time of the Disruption, because Judah was the royal tribe, of which the Christ was to come. The history of the Northern Kingdom is omitted by the chronicler.

Then, again, all that pertains to worship is here emphasized; the Temple and its services, priests, Levites, singers, and the hatefulness of idolatry. It is shown that the troubles of the nation were due to their disregard of the claims of Jehovah, and their prosperity was due to their return to Him. The Kings are political and royal, but the Chronicles are sacred and ecclesiastical.

There are some numerical inconsistencies in these records, due, no doubt, to the imperfect state of some of the Hebrew manuscripts, but the many alleged contradictions and errors cannot be proved.

Although we show the parallel passages in Kings and Chronicles in the 2 Kings Analysis, we here present an analysis of each of the latter records.

# Analysis of 1 Chronicles

## I. GENEALOGICAL TABLES (chs. 1–9)

### 1. The Primeval Period       1:1–23
Adam to Abraham

### 2. The Patriarchal Period       1:24–2:2
Abraham to Jacob

### 3. The National Period       2:3–9:44
Posterity of Jacob's Sons

## II. KINGS OF ISRAEL (chs. 10–29)

### 1. The End of Saul's Reign (ch. 10)

### 2. The Whole of David's Reign (11–29:30)

| | | |
|---|---|---|
| (i.) Prominent Events | | 11–22 |
| (a) | His Followers | (11–12) |
| (b) | His Enterprises | (13–17) |
| (c) | His Conflicts | (18–20) |
| (d) | His Failure | (21) |
| (e) | His Charges | (22) |

**3. The Beginning of Solomon's Reign (29:22b–25)**

# Analysis of 2 Chronicles

## I. THE REIGN OF SOLOMON (chs. 1–9)

**1. The Beginning (1:1–13)**

**2. The Progress (1:14–9:12)**

## II. THE KINGS OF JUDAH (10–36:21)

# 17

# Ezra

Keyword: reconstruction
Chapters: 10
Date: 536–458 BC
78 years

The closing verses of 2 Chronicles are also the opening verses of this book, and there are other evidences of the same compiler. The period represented is from the close of the captivity to the reformation under Ezra in 458 BC.

Ezra appears as the writer of chapter 9, and, in all likelihood was the compiler of the whole book, though in parts of it he is spoken of in the third person.

It is important to observe that this book is a compilation, and not a single narrative, and it is interesting to see what are its component parts. Of its 880 verses, 109 are narrative, 111 are registers, 44 are letters, 3 are a proclamation, 3 are an excerpt, and 10 are a prayer. Furthermore, it should be noted that a sizeable number of verses, 4:8–6:18; 7:12–26, are in Aramaic.

Chronicles, Ezra, Esther, and Nehemiah are ecclesiastical history, concerned almost exclusively with the institutional religion of Judah, and, although there may have been later additions to this history, it may well have been given its present form by Ezra, who was an instructor in the Law of God.

The Babylonian Empire was succeeded by the Medo-Persian Empire in 536 BC, whereupon Cyrus offered the Jews their liberty (1:2–4), and the number of those who availed themselves of the privilege under the leadership of Zerubbabel and Jeshua is recorded in much of this book. In keeping with the religious purpose of this history, we are told that the first thing they did was to build the altar of Burnt Offering, and then the Temple (ch. 3). The work was hindered by opposition (ch. 4), but in consequence of the inspirational ministries of Haggai and Zechariah the Lord's House was completed in 516 BC, twenty years after the return from Babylon (6:15). With this chapter (6) ends the first division of the book, and between it and the next chapter (7) is a period of 58 years, 516–458 BC, to which belongs the story of Esther. Also in this period occurred the battles of Marathon, Thermopylae, and Salamis; and the deaths of Confucius and Buddha.

In the second division of the book (chs. 8–10) is the personal history of Ezra's journey to Jerusalem, with commission from Artaxerxes Longimanus in 458 BC, and his exertions for the reformation of the people.

During the period covered by chapter 4 of Ezra belong chapters 10–12 of Daniel. The things to be specifically noted in this record are: the Decree of Cyrus (1:2–4); the erection of the altar and foundation of the Temple (ch. 3); Haggai and Zechariah (5:1); the letter of Darius (6:6–12); Ezra's prayer (9:6–15); the Gentile kings, Cyrus (ch. 1), Darius I (ch. 6), and Artaxerxes (ch. 7).

# Analysis of Ezra

## I. THE RETURN FROM CAPTIVITY, UNDER ZERUBBABEL
Chapters 1–6 20 years

### 1. Restoration of the Jews (chs. 1–2)
(i.)   Restoration. The Decree of Cyrus                    1
(ii.)  Registration. The Return of the Captives            2

### 2. Opposition to the Work (chs. 3–4)
(i.)   Reconstruction. The Sacrifices Renewed and the Temple Foundation Laid.                        3
(ii.)  Opposition. The Samaritans Resist, and the Work of Building Stopped.                           4

### 3. Dedication of the Temple (chs. 5–6)
(i.)   Investigation. The Inquiry of Tatnai and the Decree of Darius.                                 5
(ii.)  Consummation. The Completion of the Temple and Observance of the Passover.                     6
       (Haggai and Zechariah 1–8 here)

(Between Chapters 6 and 7: 58 years. Book of Esther.)

## II. RETURN FROM CAPTIVITY, UNDER EZRA
Chapters 7–10  1 year

1. The Proclamation of Artaxerxes                          7
2. The Liberation of the Jews                              8
3. The Intercession of Ezra                                9
4. The Reformation of the People                          10

# 18

# Esther

Keyword: providence
Chapters: 10
Date: 484–465 BC
20 years

When this story was written, and by whom, are un-known. Its place is between chapters six and seven of the book of Ezra, and it represents a period of about twenty years (484–465 BC).

Without justification, it has been spoken of as 'full of improbabilities or impossibilities,' and as being 'the most unchristian of Old Testament books'. It and Ruth are the only books in the Bible which bear the name of a woman.

The narrative owes much, it would seem, to Persian records. Evidence of this may be seen in details, such as the names of Haman's sons, in Esther being called 'the queen', and Mordecai, 'the Jew', and in the particulars which are given about Ahasuerus. There are references to Persian etiquette; many Persian customs and phrases are explained, and the Persian king is referred to over one hundred and eighty times.

It is said that the name of God does not occur in the story, a statement which both is and is not true. God is here in mystery, though not in manifestation.

The objection to the book, that the divine name does not occur in it, itself gives us the key to it. God's actions are manifest, but He Himself is veiled. Further, it has been shown that the incommunicable Name, or Tetragrammaton, Y.H.V.H, which stand in the Hebrew for Yahweh (Jehovah), occurs in this narrative four times in acrostic form, and at the critical points in the story (1:20; 5:4,13; 7:7), a fact which cannot possibly be of chance, but of divine design, and which demonstrates, as hardly anything else could, the outstanding truth of divine providence.

Comparatively speaking, not many of the captive Jews returned under the Edict of Cyrus, not more than 50,000, and, perhaps, 600 when Ezra returned about seventy years later. Most of the captives were born in Babylonia, and the conditions of life and business for them there were such as to disincline them to cross the desert and begin all over again in the land of their fathers. Had they all gone back under Zerubbabel, the book of Esther could not have been written. Several things in the story should be specially noted.

1) Ahasuerus is the Xerxes of classic fame (484–464 BC), who attacked the Greeks by land, and lost at Thermopylae; and by sea, and lost in the battle of Salamis. It was on his return from these defeats that he married Esther.
2) The institution of the Feast of Purim (9:26).
3) The characters of the cousins Mordecai and Esther, and of Haman.
4) The lessons of providence and retribution.

# Analysis of Esther

## I. THE GRAVE DANGER TO THE JEWS
### Chapters 1–4

## II. THE GREAT DELIVERANCE OF THE JEWS
### Chapters 5–10

# 19

# Nehemiah

Keyword: reformation
Chapters: 13
Date: 445–420 BC
25 years

In Nehemiah, as in Ezra, there are parts which are written in the first person, and, no doubt, Nehemiah himself was the author of these, though there is evidence of much later addition (e.g. Jaddua, 12:11,22, 351–331 BC). With this book Old Testament history ends.

Zerubbabel went to Jerusalem in 536 BC, and effected religious reforms. Eighty years later, in 458 BC, Ezra went to Jerusalem and effected ethical reforms. Twelve years later, in 445 BC, Nehemiah went to Jerusalem and effected civil reforms. From Zerubbabel's return to Nehemiah's was about ninety years. Of the twelve years between Ezra's and Nehemiah's returns, Professor Sayce says:

> Megabyzos the satrap of Syria, had successfully defied the Persian king, and forced him to agree to his own terms of peace, thus giving the first open sign of the internal decay

of the Empire. It is possible that the disaffection of the satrap may account for the silence in Scripture as to the events which followed Ezra's reform. Deprived of the royal support, he would no longer be able to maintain himself as governor in face of the opposition he was certainly to experience from the Samaritans. It would also account for the condition in which we find the Jews when the book of Nehemiah opens. The walls of the city are still unbuilt, Ezra has ceased to be governor, the people are in great affliction and reproach, the Arabs are encamping close to Jerusalem, Sanballat and his allies are all-powerful, and priests and laity alike have gone back to their heathen and foreign wives.

The story in Nehemiah is full of rapid movement and vigorous energy. Action and unction everywhere characterise it, because there move to and fro two men on whom in a wonderful degree rested the Spirit of God. The narrative opens in the twentieth year of the reign of Artaxerxes Longimanus, and ends in the reign of Darius II.

In this book we have an excellent autobiography. Nehemiah is a great character, courageous, resolute, and energetic; an untiring worker, and a model organizer. Dr A.T. Pierson has analysed his method under five points – division of labour, adaptation of work and worker, honesty and economy in administration, co-operation in labour, and concentration at any assaulted point. Nehemiah's personal diary in chapters 1–7, should be frequently read.

Outstanding passages are those which record Nehemiah's conflict with his enemies; his great lead as a governor (ch. 5); the reading of the Law (ch. 8); the prayer of the Levites (ch. 9); and the correction of abuses (ch. 13). In this enterprise Malachi was to Nehemiah what Haggai and Zechariah had been to Ezra.

# Analysis of Nehemiah

## I. THE CONSTRUCTION OF THE WALL
(chs. 1–7)

### 1. Preparation for the Effort (chs. 1–2)
| | | |
|---|---|---|
| (i.) | News from Jerusalem | 1:1–3 |
| (ii.) | Nehemiah's Prayer | 1:4–11 |
| (iii.) | Request and Response | 2:1–9 |
| (iv.) | Arrival at Jerusalem | 2:10–20 |

### 2. Reconstruction of the Wall (ch. 3)
| | |
|---|---|
| (i.) | The Work Organised |
| (ii.) | The Labour Distributed |

### 3. Opposition to the Project (4–6:14)
| | | |
|---|---|---|
| (i.) | External Difficulties | 4, 6:1–14 |
| (ii.) | Internal Difficulties | 5 |

### 4. Completion of the Task (6:15–7:3)
| | | |
|---|---|---|
| (i.) | Enemies Discouraged | 6:15–19 |
| (ii.) | Gates Guarded | 7:1–3 |

## II. THE CONSECRATION OF THE PEOPLE
(chs. 8–10)

### 1. Revival of Religion (ch. 8)
| | | |
|---|---|---|
| (i.) | The Book of the Law Read | 8:1–12 |
| (ii.) | The Feast of Tabernacles Kept | 8:13–18 |

### 2. Confession of the People (ch. 9)

### 3. Renewal of the Covenant (ch. 10)

# III. THE CONSOLIDATION OF THE WORK
## (chs. 11–13)

## 1. Distribution of the People (11–12:26)

## 2. Dedication of the Wall (12:27–13:3)

## 3. Correction of Abuses (13:4–31)

# The Poetical Writings

# 20

# Introduction

We have included only the Psalms, the Song of Songs, and Lamentations in this group, but much of what passes for prose in the Scriptures is in reality poetry. This is true of large portions of the prophetical writings, and parts of the gospels and the epistles. Furthermore, poetry is to be found scattered throughout the prose of the Old Testament, as for example in Genesis 4:23,24; Exodus 15; Numbers 31:14,15,17,18,27–30; Judges 5; 2 Samuel 1:17–27. Poetic forms are manifold, and there are many of these in the Bible, as, for example, the ode, the elegy, the lyric, the idyll, the epic, and the drama. Job is dramatic, the Psalms are lyrical, and the Song of Songs is elegiac.

English poetry depends largely for its effect upon the recurrence of sound, but Hebrew poetry cultivates the recurrence of thought. This is the parallelistic method, and is of many varieties, such as the synonymous, antithetic, synthetic, introverted, iterative, responsory, alternate, and climacteric, all of which forms are to be found in the Psalter. The acrostic device is also found in Hebrew poetry, in Lamentations, and some of the psalms. Poetic form in the Scriptures is important for interpretation, and unless the structure of a passage is discerned, its meaning may easily be missed. It's useful to remember also that poetry must be read as poetry, and not as history, or as doctrine.

# 21

# The Psalms

Keyword: experience
Hymns: 150

The Psalter is the hymn book of the Hebrews, and a hymn book does not lend itself to formal analysis. Each psalm may do so, to some extent, but the whole collection allows only of certain classifications, which, however, are of considerable value.

*Divisions*
The Psalter is in five parts or books, each of which, except the last, ends with a doxology of a liturgical character. These divisions are: 1–41; 42–72; 73–89; 90–106; 107–150.

*Authorship*
Of the 150 psalms, 100 are, by their titles, related to authors. Of these 73 are assigned to David, 10 to the School of Korah, 12 to the School of Asaph, 2 to Solomon, 1 to Ethan, 1 to Heman, 1 to Moses, and 50 are anonymous. The seventieth mentions Jeremiah as the author of Psalm 87, and Haggai and Zechariah as

the authors of Psalms 96 and 97; and it is quite likely that Ezra wrote Psalm 69, and that Hezekiah wrote Psalms 70–86 (Isa. 38:20). These particulars provide a basis for investigation as to authorship.

## Date
It is impossible with any precision to fix dates to most of the Psalms, but it may with confidence be stated that the great song period in Israel's history was the three hundred years from David's time to the time of Hezekiah. In the Psalter are songs, which belong to the period before and after this, but the majority are to be placed within those limits.

## Prefixes
All the Psalms have some title except the following thirty-four: 1, 2, 10, 33, 43, 71, 91, 93–97, 99, 104–107, 111–119, 135–137, 146–150. Of those titled, fourteen bear the name of David, and claim to be related to certain events in his varied career (7, 59, 56, 34, 52, 57, 142, 54, 18, 60, 51, 3, 63, 30). Though these prefixes may be helpful, they are not authoritative.

## Divine Titles
Everywhere in the Bible, divine names or titles represent divine qualities, attributes, and attitudes, and their occurrence has both a chronological and a theological value. The following chart shows what divine names or titles occur in the Psalter, and where.

| Book | I | II | III | IV | V |
|------|-----|-----|-----|-----|-----|
| Adon | 2 | 1 | – | 1 | 5 |
| Adonai | 13 | 18 | 15 | 1 | 12 |
| Jah | – | – | 2 | 7 | 32 |
| Jehovah | 275 | 32 | 44 | 106 | 236 |
| El | 18 | 16 | 20 | 9 | 10 |
| Elohim | 50 | 198 | 60 | 18 | 30 |
| Eloah | 1 | 1 | – | – | 2 |
| Elyon | 3 | 4 | 5 | 4 | 1 |
| Shaddai | – | 1 | 1 | 1 | – |
| | | | | | |
| Psalms | 1–41 | 42–72 | 73–89 | 90–106 | 107–150 |

The Hebrews never thought of God in an abstract way; to them He was a divine being, living and active, transcendent and yet immanent. They believed also that God was One, and was from everlasting. On God's personality, unity, and eternity the Bible revelation rests, and this triple truth is in the very substance of Psalms.

*Classifications*
These Hebrew songs may be classified in many ways, and such groupings are eminently suggestive and instructive. The following are a few suggested classifications:

| | |
|---|---|
| Messianic psalms | 16, 22, 24, 40, 68, 69, 118. |
| Penitential psalms | 6, 32, 38, 51, 102, 130, 143. |
| Hallelujah psalms | 106, 111, 112, 113, 117, 135, 146–150. |
| Didactic psalms | 1, 5, 7, 15, 17, 50, 73, 94, 101. |
| Pilgrim psalms | 120–134. |

| Prayer psalms | 17, 86, 90, 102, 142. |
| Royal psalms | 92–100. |
| Devotional psalms | 3, 16, 54, 61, 86, 28, 41, 59, 70, 67, 122, 144. |
| Morning psalms | 3–5, 19, 57, 63, 108. |
| Evening psalms | 4, 8, 143. |
| Meditation psalms | 16, 56, 60. |
| Trouble psalms | 4, 5, 11, 28, 41, 55, 59, 64, 109, 120, 140, 143. |
| Prophetical psalms | 2, 16, 22, 40, 45, 68, 69, 72, 97, 110, 118. |
| Historical psalms | 78, 105, 106. |

*Selected Studies*
Some, if not all, of the above classifications lend themselves to profoundly instructive development, from which I select one for the purpose of illustration, the Messiah (pages 92, 93).

*Prophetical Psalms*
That there is a prophetic element in the Psalter will not seriously be called into question, for indeed, as Westcott says,

> A Divine counsel was wrought out in the course of the life of Israel. We are allowed to see in 'the people of God' signs of the purpose of God for humanity. The whole history is prophetic. It is not enough to recognise that the Old Testament contains prophecies; the Old Testament is one vast prophecy.

We may say that the three strands which make the web of Hebrew prophecy relate to the Messiah, Israel, and the Gentiles. All three are found in the Psalter, and it must be evident that they are vitally related to one another. Messiah is the hope of the world, and Israel is the medium of the divine revelation and mission, 'the instrument for accomplishing the world-wide extension of His kingdom'.

The time is predicted when all nations shall acknowledge Christ's sovereignty (22:27; 65:2,5; 66:4; 68:29–33; 86:9; 102:15,22; 138:4). Examine these and related passages carefully.

That this consummation is to be reached through Israel does not need to be argued. Whatever may be one's view of the Messianic kingdom of the future, whether it be regarded as visible, or as only spiritual, no one can question that Israel, through whom Christ came, and from whom we have received the Bible, has been chosen of God for its realisation, and there is abundant evidence in the Scriptures that this race has been preserved by God for the fulfilment of the Abrahamic covenant (68; 88; 102:13–16; 96–98). This implies, of course, Israel's own restoration and felicity in the future, of which Psalm 126, beyond any past fulfilment, may be regarded as a prophecy.

But behind and beneath Israelitish and Gentile prophecy is Messianic prophecy, of which the Psalter is full. We have Christ's own warrant for looking for Him in the Psalms, for He said: 'All things must be fulfilled which were written in ... the Psalms concerning Me' (Lk. 24:44), and on several occasions He interpreted of Himself passages in the Psalter. Compare, e.g. Psalm 118:22 with Matthew 21:42; and Psalm 110:1 with Matthew 22:42–45 (*et al.*). Christ's apostles also make this use of the Psalms, cf. Acts 4:11 and 1 Peter 2:7, with Psalm 118:22; John 2:17, with Psalm 69:9; and Matthew 13:35, with Psalm 78:2 (*et al.*).

The Messianic reference in some of the psalms must be obvious to all who read, but far more numerous are references which are not so obvious, but which the New Testament warrants us in regarding as Messianic.

These references tell of His manhood, 8:4,5 (Heb. 2:6–8); His sonship, 2:7 (Heb. 1:5); 110:1 (Mt. 22:42–45); His deity, 45:6,11 (Heb. 1:8); His holiness, 45:7; 89:18,19 (Heb. 1:9); His priesthood, 110:4 (Heb. 5:6); His kingship, 2:6; 89:18,19,27 (Acts 5:31; Rev. 19:16); His conquests, 105:5,6 (Rev. 6:17); His eternity, 61:6,7; 45:17; 72:17; 102:25–27 (Heb. 1:10); His universal sovereignty, 72:8; 103:19 (Rev. 19:16); His obedience 40:6–8 (Heb. 10:5–7); His zeal, 69:9 (John 2:17); His sufferings, 69:9 (Rev. 15:3); His betrayal, 41:9 (Lk. 22:48); His death, 22:1–21 (gospels); His resurrection, 2:7; 16:10 (Acts 13:33–36); His ascension, 68:18 (Eph. 4:8); and His coming again to judge, 96–98 (2 Thess. 1:7–9). These, and other such references, may be classified in various ways, but, in the main, the Messianic prophecies tell of His person, God, and man; of His character, righteous and holy; of His work, death and resurrection; and of His offices, priest, judge, and king. A mine of instruction on this whole subject will be found in Bishop Alexander's Bampton Lectures (1876), *The Witness of the Psalms to Christ and Christianity*.

## Values

In addition to the above are other values in the Psalter – it is most profitable to trace literary, imaginative, ethical, prophetical, religious, and devotional values. No part of the Bible has made a more universal appeal than has the Psalter, and it is noteworthy that out of a total of 283 direct citations from the Old Testament in the New, 116 are from Psalms. Here, as Calvin has said, 'The Holy Spirit has represented to the life all the griefs, sorrows, fears, doubts, hopes, cares, anxieties, in short, all the stormy emotions by which human minds are wont to be agitated.' Other parts of divine revelation represent God as speaking to man, but here, man is represented as speaking to God. As a devotional handbook there is nothing else like it in the world.

*Subjects*
As a guide to the reading of the psalms, the following titles may prove helpful.

1. Two Portraits.
2. God's King.
3. God My Help.
4. Before Going to Bed.
5. Talk and Walk.
6. Appeal and Answer.
7. Not Guilty.
8. Man the Viceroy of God.
9. The Righteous and the Wicked.
10. The Perils of the Pilgrim.
11. Why Flee?
12. God's Word and Man's.
13. From Sighing to Singing.
14. The Natural Man.
15. God's Guests.
16. God–satisfied.
17. At the Throne of Grace.
18. The Hebrew *Te Deum*.
19. God Has Spoken.
20. Before the Battle.
21. After the Battle.
22. The Sob and the Song.
23. All I Want.
24. Holy Worshippers.

25.　The Simple Trust of an Uplifted Soul.
26.　The Claim to Integrity.
27.　Faith and Fear.
28.　Answered Prayer.
29.　A Terrific Thunderstorm.
30.　Deliverance and Gratitude.
31.　Mingled Emotions.
32.　The Way and Blessedness of Forgiveness.
33.　The God of Creation and of History.
34.　Thanksgiving for Deliverance.
35.　A Cry for Help.
36.　Blackness and Brightness.
37.　A Problem of Providence Propounded.
38.　Sin, Suffering, and Supplication.
39.　Trust in Trial.
40.　Reminiscence and Request.
41.　Triumph Over Trouble.
42.　Laughter Through Tears.
43.　Laughter Through Tears.
44.　Intellectual and Moral Perplexity.
45.　A Nuptial Ode.
46.　Rock–Safe.
47.　The Great King.
48.　Broken Bondage.
49.　Worthless Worldly Wealth.
50.　A Vision of Judgment.
51.　Sorry.
52.　The Treacherous Tongue.
53.　The Futility of Evil.
54.　Deliverance for the Devout.
55.　An Ode of the Oppressed.
56.　Peace in a Plight.
57.　The Faith of a Fugitive.
58.　The Character and Destiny of Wicked Judges.
59.　Inward Victory over Outward Enemies.

95.    Privilege and Peril.
96.    A Missionary Melody.
97.    The King and the Kingdom.
98.    The Universal King is Crowned.
99.    The Character of the King.
100.   The God to Praise.
101.   Integrity Within and Without.
102.   The Transient Life and the Abiding Lord.
103.   The World Within.
104.   The World Without.
105.   How the Lord Treated Israel.
106.   How Israel Treated the Lord.
107.   A Song of the Redeemed.
108.   Praise for Victory.
109.   Solemn Execration.
110.   The Priest-King.
111.   The Lord Who is to be Feared.
112.   The Man who Fears the Lord.
113.   Glory and Grace.
114.   A Song of the Exodus.
115.   God and Idols.
116.   Gratitude for Deliverance.
117.   A Universal Choir.
118.   A Choral Hosanna.
119.   The Law of the Lord.
120.   Peace versus War.
121.   The Keeping God.
122.   Love of the Lord's House.
123.   Uplifted Eyes.
124.   Mercy Remembered.
125.   Confidence in God.
126.   Seedtime and Harvest.
127.   Toil and Home.
128.   Family Felicity.
129.   The Vindication of the Righteous.

# 22

# Song of Solomon

This book has always been ranked among the Canonical Writings of the Old Testament, and the universal voice of antiquity ascribes it to Solomon. In the Hebrew canon the Song belongs to the third division, the Hagiographa, and is the first of the five Megilloth, or 'Rolls', the others being Ruth, Lamentations, Ecclesiastes, and Esther.

Peculiar difficulties beset the interpretation of the writing, and we should at least be tolerant of wide differences of opinion. It is never referred to in the other books of the Old Testament, nor in the Old Testament Apocrypha, nor in the New Testament, nor in Philo, nor in Josephus; and the name of God does not appear in it. I am only stating these facts, and not drawing any inferences from them.

Many interpretations have been assigned to this biblical marriage poem, which may be summarised as follows:

1. That it was written to celebrate the marriage of Solomon with Pharaoh's daughter.
2. That it is an account in song of how Solomon wooed and won a fair maiden from the Lebanon hills, and of their mutual love.

3. That it sets forth the true devotion of a youth and a maiden in humble life, in spite of the attempt made by Solomon to turn the heart of the latter to himself.
4. That it is a collection of several independent poems (Budde distinguishes twenty-three) on the subject of love.
5. That it is not historical, but allegorical, depicting (i.) the history of the Jews from Abraham to the Messiah; (ii.) the deliverance of Israel from Egypt, their wilderness wanderings, and their entrance into Canaan; (iii.) the union of Jehovah with ancient Israel; (iv.) the union of Christ and the Church; and (v.) the love-life of the soul and the Lord.

Difficulties accompany each of these interpretations, and it is not possible for us to say what the design of the author was, but that need not interfere with our discerning a value or values in the Song.

Our view is that here, as in Jonah, we have allegory emerging from history. As to the history, we take the view, influentially held, that in the Song there are not two, but three, chief characters, Solomon, Shulamith, and a shepherd lover. The story briefly is this: a beautiful country girl from Shulam (i.e., Shunem, 5 miles north of Jezreel) was surprised by the king on one of his journeys to the north (6:11f), was brought to Jerusalem and placed in the royal palace (1:4b,5), where, as the poem opens, the ladies of the harem ('daughters of Jerusalem') are singing the praises of Solomon. The king himself makes great efforts to win the affection of the Shulamite (1:9, etc.); but she remains faithful to the memory of her shepherd lover (1:7, etc.), who at last appears, and is allowed by the magnanimous monarch to return to his mountain home with his bride (8:5ff).

George Saintsbury has called the climax of this story (8:6,7) perfect English prose.

As to the *allegory*, what is literal may well point to something spiritual, and the Song has always been read in this way by mystic saints, such as Bernard of Clairvaux, who preached eighty-six sermons on the first two chapters, and McCheyne, and Spurgeon. If we regard the king in the poem as the world, the shepherd-lover as Christ, and the Shulamite as the individual soul, we shall not fail to be helped.

In the face of all the world's allurements we are expected by our Lord, the 'Lover of our souls', to be faithful to Him, and one day He will consummate His love for us in glory.

# Analysis of the Song of Solomon

## A – LOVE'S FIRST ENTRANCING DAYS
### Chapters 1:2–5:1

### Part I. The Wedding Day (1:2–2:7)
1. The Bridal Pair and the Daughters of Jerusalem approaching the Palace     1:2–4
2. The Apologies and Memories of the New Queen     1:5–8
3. In the Banqueting House – The Love of Espousals     1:9–l4
4. In the Bridal Chamber – The Felicity of Wedlock     1:15–2:7

### Part II. The Courtship Days (2:8–3:5)
5. Reminiscences of a Visit of the Beloved at the Springtide of Love     2:8–17

# 23

# The Lamentations

Keyword: disconsolate
Chapters: 5

This is an acrostic dirge, written by Jeremiah, rhapsodic in character, and of great beauty and pathos.

The occasion of it was the destruction of Jerusalem and its Temple by Nebuchadnezzar in 586 BC. The writing is one of the 'Rolls' (see chapter on Song of Songs).

Its form is well worthy of careful examination. There are five complete poems, represented by our chapters. In each of the first, second, fourth, and fifth are 22 verses, corresponding to the number of letters in the Hebrew alphabet, and in the third are three times twenty-two. In the first, second, and fourth poems, each verse begins with a letter of the Hebrew alphabet in order (e.g., 1, a; 2, b; 3, c; etc.), and in poem five there are three verses to each letter (e.g., 1–3, a, a, a; 4–6, b, b, b, etc.), and in poem five, though there are just the 22 verses, the acrostic is dropped. Further, in the first and second and third poems there are three clauses to each verse, but in the third poem there is an acrostic initial to each clause. The fourth poem has only couplets; and the fifth drops both acrostic structure and dirge rhythm (see *Moulton's Modern Reader's Bible*). Taken together, these poems enforce the exhortation of Hebrews 12:5, and were designed to teach the Jews neither to 'despise the chastening of the Lord,' nor to 'faint' when 'rebuked of Him' (cf. Lk. 19:41,42).

Jeremiah's vision of Jerusalem wasted and Babylon exulting should be compared with John's vision of Babylon destroyed and the New Jerusalem revealed in triumph and heavenly beauty (Rev. 18, 21, 22). Better to be one with Jerusalem in afflictions that issue in glory, than one with Babylon in the pride that ends in shame.

# Analysis of the Lamentations

## I. THE CONDITION OF MISERY IN ZION
### Chapter 1

1. The Prophet's Description                     1–11
2. The People's Reflection                       12–22

## II. THE CAUSE OF ZION'S OVERTHROW
### Chapter 2

1. What the Lord wrought against her             1–10
2. Why the Lord wrought against her              11–22

## III. THE DESIGN OF ZION'S AFFLICTION
### Chapter 3

1. Calamity and Consolation                      1–39
2. Confession and Confidence                     40–66

## IV. ZION'S REMEMBRANCE OF FORMER DAYS
Chapter 4

## V. THE APPEAL OF ZION TO GOD
Chapter 5

# The Wisdom Writings

The Wisdom Writings

# 24

# Introduction

Four types of mind are recognised in the Bible, which account for four kinds of literature – the priest, the poet, the prophet, and the philosopher (cf. Jer. 18:18). It is the last of these we are now to consider, from whom we receive the Wisdom Literature.

> Side by side with prophets defending the theocracy, and singers taking their inspiration from the Temple service, with historians compiling annals of kings, and scribes expounding the Law, there was a class of wise men, who had habits of thought and forms of literature peculiar to themselves (Prof R. Moulton).

This type has adorned the letters of every great people, as may be seen by reference to Ptahhotep in Egypt, Epictetus in Greece, Marcus Aurelius in Rome, Alexander Pope in England, and Benjamin Franklin in America. We need not be surprised then, to find Wisdom Literature in the Bible. It is found in brief in scattered places in the form of riddle (Judg. 14:14), fable (Judg. 9:8,15), maxim (Eccles. 4:9–12), epigram (Prov. 23:1–3), sonnet (Prov. 4:10–19), dramatic monologue (Prov. 1:20–33),

and proverb (Prov. 22:1); and in elaborated form in
Job and Ecclesiastes, and in the non-canonical books
Ecclesiasticus and the Wisdom of Solomon. Nor is this
kind of literature confined to the pre-Christian period,
for it is represented in the New Testament by parts of
the Sermon on the Mount, the parables, and the Epistle
of James. In all likelihood there were of old, schools of
wisdom in which the ancients taught their pupils (cf. 1
Sam. 24:13; Job 12:12), and, it would appear, wise men
sat for this purpose at the gate of the city (Prov. 31:23).
Pre-eminent among the wise was Solomon, who is said
to have composed 1005 songs and 3000 proverbs (1
Kings 4:29–34).

Prophet, priest, and philosopher approached the
same subject from different angles. Of righteousness,
the prophet would say, 'It is just'; the priest would
say, 'It is commanded'; but the philosopher would say,
'It is prudent.' Of sin, the prophet would say, 'It is
disobedience'; the priest would say, 'It is defilement';
but the philosopher would say, 'It is folly.' The wise
men were observers of life, and the Wisdom books are
the product of their analytic observations. To remember
this will help us to understand why there is scarcely
any reference in these Writings to Israel, or the Temple,
or the Messianic hope (cf. Prov. 8:22–31).

The simplest form of wisdom in the Bible is in what
we call the book of Proverbs; and the most elaborate
form is in Ecclesiastes, where reflective analysis is
turned upon the sum of things, and in Job, where we
have dramatized a philosophical discussion on the
problem of suffering. Job may equally well be classified
as poetical, for it contains specimens of all the three
main elements of poetry – epic, lyric, and dramatic
composition.

# 25

# Job

Keyword: tested
Chapters: 42

The author of this writing is unknown, as are the time of writing and the period in which Job lived. That the hero of the poem was a real person and not the creation of imagination is evident from such references as Ezek. 14:14,20; Jas. 5:11; as also from internal evidence.

The dramatic form in which the story is cast in no way invalidates its historical trustworthiness.

So little is there in the poem to indicate the age in which Job lived that opinions have varied by as much as one thousand years. Some take the view that he lived before Abraham, and would place the story between the eleventh and twelfth chapter of Genesis; and others would place him in the captivity or post-captivity period. This shows that the value of the book is quite independent of date, and is indeed, as to its great message, dateless.

The first thing that claims our attention is the form of the story. There are epic and lyric elements in the composition, but the poem is a magnificent drama, in which no element of dramatic effect is wanting. The analysis which follows makes this evident.

This book might well be placed with the Poetical Writings, for, as to its form, it is a poem, but having regard for its theme, we place it with the Wisdom Writings, with the Proverbs and Ecclesiastes. These three books deal with the fundamental principles of the Bible, and of all religious philosophy. Proverbs declares that wisdom, or 'fear of the Lord', is the true blessedness. To this proposition there appear to be two exceptions; the one is set forth in Job, and the other in Ecclesiastes. In Job we see a man who 'was perfect and upright; one that feared God, and eschewed evil,' and yet he suffered great adversity. In Ecclesiastes we see a man, Solomon, who from being the wisest of men, became the worst, who did not fear God, and yet prospered. Solomon's conclusion was, 'All is vanity'; but Job's conclusion was, 'The fear of the Lord, that is wisdom' (Job 28:28; cf. Prov. 1:7; 15:33). The mistake of Satan was in thinking that Job served God for what he could get. The mistake of Job's wife was in thinking that with the loss of the visible and human all was lost. The mistake of Job's friends was in thinking that Job's suffering was the direct outcome of his sin. The mistake of Elihu was in thinking that he was right, and that all the others were wrong; and the mistake of Job was in thinking that God was unkind. The problem of pain is not solved in this book, but we are shown what kind of a God God is. We are shown first His power in creation, and man's weakness; and then, His wisdom in government, and man's ignorance. At the end of the mighty drama, Satan is routed, the friends are rebuked, and Job is rewarded. 'The Eternal does not answer our insistent questions; God does not explain, but He does give to the anguished spirit such a sense of the divine greatness that questioning ceases in the peace of submission.'

Then, the poem has manifold values. There is a philosophic value in its discussion of the underlying meaning of life as a whole; a scientific value in its observation of nature; a prophetical value in its authoritative divine message; a biographical value in its delineation of character; a rhetorical value in its many and marvellous speeches; a historical value in its references to places, people, and customs; a literary value in its whole conception and form; a providential value in its view that God allows His people to suffer for their good; a spiritual value in its revelation of another world and super-human beings; and a practical value in its teaching on fearing and trusting God.

The theme of the drama is 'The Mystery of Suffering', or 'The Problem of Pain', and in the discussion of this are introduced God, Satan, Job, the friends, and Elihu. The prose prologue begins with Job and God, and the prose epilogue ends with them, and between the prologue and the epilogue is the drama, describing the struggle. This book, it has been said, is a key to the whole Bible, and to man's history from creation to completed redemption.

1. Humans unfallen and tried.
2. Sinning and suffering.
3. Seeking human help in legality, morality, philosophy.
4. Needing and receiving a revelation from God.
5. Humbled, penitent, believing.
6. Restored to a better estate than at first.

The poem teaches that suffering is not always penal and retributive, but may be, and sometimes is, disciplinary and educative.

Of Job, Thomas Carlyle said,

I call this book, apart from all theories about it, one of the
grandest things ever written with pen. One feels, indeed, as
if it were not Hebrew; such a noble universality, different
from noble patriotism or sectarianism, reigns in it. A noble
book, all men's book! It is our first, oldest statement of the
never ending problem—man's destiny, and God's ways
with him here in this earth. And all in such free, flowing
outlines; grand in its sincerity, in its simplicity, and its epic
melody, and repose of reconcilement. There is the seeing
eye, the mildly understanding heart. So true every way;
true insight and vision for all things; material things no
less than spiritual . . . Such living likenesses were never
since drawn. Sublime sorrow, sublime reconciliation;
oldest choral melody as of the heart of mankind; so soft,
and great; as the summer midnight, as the world with its
seas and stars! There is nothing written, I think, in the
Bible or out of it, of equal literary merit.

# Analysis of Job

## THE PROLOGUE (chs. 1–2. Prose)

## 1. Job's Circumstances Before his Trial (1:1–5)

## 2. The First Assault (1:6–22)
| | | |
|---|---|---|
| (i.) | Satan and Jehovah | 1:6–12 |
| (ii.) | Job's Afflictions and Integrity | 1:13–22 |

## 3. The Second Assault (2:1–10)
| | | |
|---|---|---|
| (i.) | Satan and Jehovah | 2:1–6 |
| (ii.) | Job's Afflictions and Integrity | 2:7–10 |

## 4. The Coming and Conduct of Job's Friends (2:11-13)

## THE DRAMA (3-42:6)

### 1. The Lamentation of Job (ch. 3)
(i.)    'Why was I born?'
(ii.)   'Why did I not die in infancy?'
(iii.)  'Why is life prolonged?'

### 2. The Discussion of the Friends (chs. 4-31)
(i.) First Cycle                                    4-14
     *Eliphaz* (4-5)        *Job* (6-7)
     *Bildad* (8)           *Job* (9-10)
     *Zophar* (11)          *Job* (12-14)

(ii.) Second Cycle                                  15-21
     *Eliphaz* (15)         *Job* (16-17)
     *Bildad* (18)          *Job* (19)
     *Zophar* (20)          *Job* (21)

(iii.) Third Cycle                                  22-31
     *Eliphaz* (22)         *Job* (23-24)
     *Bildad* (25)          *Job* (26:1-27:10)
     *Zophar* (27:11-28:28) *Job* (29-31)

### 3. The Intervention of Elihu (chs. 32-37)
     Introduction: 32:1-5
(i.)    His Speech to the Three Friends        32:6-22
(ii.)   His Speech to Job                           33
(iii.)  His Speech to the Three Friends             34
(iv.)   His Speech to Job                        35-37

## 4. The Revelation of Jehovah (38–42:6)

Jehovah (38–40:2)              Job (40:3–5)
Jehovah (40:6–41)             Job (42:1–6)

## THE EPILOGUE (42:7–17. Prose)

## 1. Jehovah's Wrath and Witness (42:7–9)

## 2. Job's Prayer and Prosperity (42:10–17)

# 26

# Proverbs

Keyword: conduct
Chapters: 31

In approaching this work we must recognise that it is different and distinct from any other book in the Bible. It is not history, nor poetry, nor rhapsody, nor prophecy, nor law, nor ritual, nor story, nor dogma; and although it belongs to the Wisdom Literature, it differs from the other books, Job and Ecclesiastes. It is unfortunate, to say the least, that this work is divided into chapters and verses, for this artificial arrangement buries literary form and hinders the appreciation of it.

*Authorship*
All we know of this is what may be learned from Proverbs itself, where are named, as responsible for the various collections: Solomon (1:1; 25:1); The Wise (22:17); Men of Hezekiah (25:1); Agur (30:1); and King Lemuel and his mother (31:1). Solomon we know, and among 'the men of Hezekiah' were probably Isaiah and Micah (cf. 2 Chron. 31:13), but of the others we have no information.

*Date*

We must distinguish between the time of the writing of these proverbs and the time of their being collected and edited. The reference to Hezekiah and his wise men 'copying out' proverbs of Solomon (25:1), indicates that in Hezekiah's time wisdom lore was being collected, and it may be that some editing was done by Ezra. In any case, these collections are the product of the schools of wisdom (see Introduction to the Wisdom Writings), and extend over a long period.

*Contents*

The book of Proverbs no more lends itself to formal analysis than does the Psalter, because of its diversified contents; it must suffice therefore to introduce it according to its character.

Like the books of Moses, the psalter, and the historical books of the New Testament, Proverbs is in five main parts, with an introduction, as follows:

## INTRODUCTION (1:1–6)

Indicating the practical purpose the collection is intended to serve.

Part I.  Chs. 1:7–9:18. Proverbs of Solomon (1:1).
         The value and attainment of true wisdom.
Part II. Chs. 10:1–22:16. Proverbs of Solomon.
         On practical morality.
Part III. Chs. 22:17–24:34. Proverbs of the Wise.
         Admonitions on the study of wisdom.
Part IV. Chs. 25–29. Proverbs of Solomon selected by
         the men of Hezekiah. Ethical and Economical.
Part V. Chs. 30–31. Words of Agur and of King
         Lemuel. Enigmatical and Domestic.

*Literary Form*

The method and form of these sayings are matched to the design, which is to state truth so briefly and vividly that it can easily be remembered. In pursuance of this, three devices are adopted: antithesis, as in 16:22; comparison, as in 17:10; and imagery, as in 27:15. The unit proverb is employed in chs. 10:1–22:16; and there are here 375 of these in couplet form, each quite distinct, though having a common thought-basis.

The proverb cluster is employed, that is, an aggregation of unit proverbs on a common theme, such as on fools (26:3–12).

The epigram is employed, that is, a unit proverb, organically enlarged, as on the transitoriness of riches (23:4,5).

The dramatic monologue is employed, wherein wisdom is personified, as in Wisdom's cry of warning (1:20–33).

And the sonnet is employed, as in the commandment and its reward (3:1–10).

Of Part II (chs. 10:1–22:16) Professor Nourse has said,

> These are not mere popular sayings, but products of fine literary workmanship . . . What we have to do with here is the choicest product of the Wisdom Schools, and presupposes long training and practice before such art could be brought to the degree of perfection we see exhibited in Proverbs.

*Themes*

The topics treated in this wonderful collection are many. Wisdom, sin, goodness, wealth, the tongue, temptation, pride, humility, justice, friendship, human freedom, idleness, poverty, education, forgiveness, folly, love, marriage, family life, pleasures, diligence, dishonesty, revenge, strife, gluttony and success are all dealt with in final forms of expression, and dynamically.

There are here also wonderful cameo pictures of social types.

> The prating fool, winking with his eye; the practical joker, as dangerous as a madman casting firebrands about; the talebearer, and the man who 'harps upon a matter', separating chief friends; the whisperer whose words are like dainty morsels going down into the innermost parts of the belly; the backbiting tongue, drawing gloomy looks all around as surely as the north wind brings rain; the false boaster, compared to wind and clouds without rain; the haste to be rich; the liberal man that scattereth and yet increaseth, while others are withholding only to come to want; the speculator holding back his corn amid the curses of the people; the man of wandering life, like a restless bird; the unsocial man that separateth himself, foregoing wisdom for the sake of his own private desire; the cheerfulness that is a continual feast.

Social problems are also to be found here, such as the relations of husband and wife, of master and servant, of parents and children, of rich and poor. Also many human experiences are reflected in these proverbs, such as care, joy, feebleness, satiety, sorrow, and so on; and although not much is said about religion, it is clear that the morality of these sayings is based upon it. Vice is condemned and virtue commended, by appeals to the highest motives (cf. 5:21; 15:11; 16:6; 19:29; 23:17–19; 26:10).

*Teaching*
The design of these proverbs is stated at the outset (1:1–6). The fundamental note of wisdom is 'the fear of the Lord' (1:7,9,10; 15:33). The teaching is positive and practical. Existing religious institutions, the Law,

priests, and sacrifices are not in view, but the tone of the teaching is definitely monotheistic; there is here no scepticism, but a sincere belief in God, and in His wise and just government of the world. If the teaching seems to be utilitarian, it is because no other than this life was in the view of the writers; they did not have the New Testament outlook upon the future.

We must be careful not to assume that all these proverbs are of unlimited and universal application; on the contrary, we can find in the Scriptures many exceptions to what is here affirmed; for example, 10:27, with Genesis 4:8, and 2 Samuel 1:23; and 16:7, with Acts 14:19. Most of the teaching of the Scriptures is relative, not absolute; and regard must always be had for whether this life only, or the next also, is in view.

# 27

# Ecclesiastes

Keyword: vanity
Chapters: 12

This book is the most mysterious in all the Bible. It has been called 'the sphinx of Hebrew literature, with its unsolved riddles of history and life'. About no biblical writing has there been such diversity of opinion as to the book's authorship, date, motive, and place. The Solomonic authorship has been, and is, stoutly defended and denied. Dates assigned for the book range over nearly a thousand years. Dogmatism and scepticism have alike claimed the author as their champion. And as to plan, some regard the book as a formal treatise, and others regard it as a collection of unconnected thoughts and maxims, like Pascal's *Pensées*, or Hare's *Guesses at Truth*.

The consideration of these matters lies outside the scope of this publication, and I have felt it best just to give a detailed analysis of the Work as it appeals to me, and to leave the reader to form his own conclusions.

Four things may safely be said of the book: (1) that it belongs to the Wisdom Literature; (2) that its theme is 'The Quest for the Chief Good'; (3) that it writes 'Vanity' on all things 'under the sun'; and (4) that the final verdict of the book is that to fear and obey God is the whole duty of man.

Of Ecclesiastes, Mr E.C. Stedman says,

> Whether prose or verse, I know nothing grander in its impassioned survey of mortal pain and pleasure, its estimate of failure and success; none of more noble sadness; no poem working more indomitably for spiritual illumination. Here, as nowhere else, immortal poetry has been made out of the body's decay (12:1–7).

## Analysis of Ecclesiastes

### Title: 1:1. Theme: 'The Chief Good' (6:12)

### I. THE PROBLEM STATED (1:2–11)

The wearisome monotony of all things human and earthly.

Affirmation (2)
Interrogation (3)
Illustration (4–11)

### II. THE PROBLEM STUDIED (1:12–12:8)

**Part 1 – Inductions (1:12–6:12)**

| | | |
|---|---|---:|
| (i.) | Koheleth's experiences | 1:12–2:26 |
| (a) | *The Quest by Wisdom and Pleasure* | (1:12–2:11) |
| | By Wisdom | 1:12–18 |
| | By Pleasure | 2:1–11 |
| (b) | *The Wise and Foolish Compared* | (2:12–23) |
| | Wisdom is better than Folly | 2:12–13 |

### III. THE PROBLEM SOLVED (12:8–14)

# The Prophetical Writings

# 28

# Introduction

There is a sense in which the whole of the Old Testament is prophetical. Bishop Westcott has said,

> The Old Testament is one vast prophecy. The application of prophetic words in each case has regard to the ideal indicated by them, and is not limited by the historical fact with which they were connected. But the history is not set aside. The history forces the reader to look beyond.

It is most important to bear this in mind, lest, on the one hand, we imagine that the prophets spoke to their own generation only, or, on the other hand, that they spoke to a future generation mainly. Neither of these views is correct. The prophets were first *forth-tellers*, addressing messages to their own people, concerning themselves, or other peoples, and then, they were *fore-tellers*, because their day was only a moment in the progress of a divine plan. The prophets had both *insight* and *foresight*, and foresight because of their insight. Theirs was a manifold function, for they combined in themselves preacher, teacher, statesman, reformer, and herald. They appeared at times of crisis in their

nation's history as the champions of righteousness;
they were essentially the moral conscience of their age.
The prophets were men of their time, and for all time.
'Holy men of God spake as they were moved by the
Holy Spirit' (2 Pet. 1:21). They were conscious of the
gift of inspiration, for one of their commonest phrases
is, 'Thus saith the Lord', but they were also conscious
that what they said had a significance beyond their
apprehension (1 Pet. 1:10,11).

The historico-predictive themes of Hebrew prophecy
are: Israel; the Gentile nations; and the Messiah, and in
the Hebrew seers we have a unique group of men, and
a unique literature. It has well been said that,

> nowhere is there to be found a succession of men like
> them in character, in vision, in eloquence. They were a
> composite of oracle, reformer, poet, and statesman. They
> uttered truth in ecstasy; the soberest judgments of a
> statesman was spoken with the passion of a reformer and
> with the lyrical cadence of poetry.

There is in the Old Testament an unmistakable development of the prophetic consciousness and message, and
while the priestly factor was always present in the life
of Israel, the prophetic factor became dominant.

Prophets and prophecy preceded the time of Samuel
(Deut. 18:15-22), but with him schools of prophets
began (1 Sam. 10:10). They were not a succession as
were the priests (cf. Amos 7:14), but they did become an
order. Their earliest work was oral, and is exemplified
in the ministry of Moses, Samuel, Elijah, Elisha, and
many minor seers; and their latest work was literary,
that is, they left written records of their preaching,
and, probably, in an instance or two, the message was
written only, and not preached. In the Hebrew Bible

the prophets are in two groups. The former prophets are the historical writings, Joshua, Judges, 1–2 Samuel, 1–2 Kings; and the latter prophets are, Isaiah, Jeremiah, Ezekiel, and the twelve minor prophets. The book of Daniel is partly historical, and partly prophetical and apocalyptical, but it was never classified with the prophets, but with another group of books called 'The Latter Writings' (Daniel; Ezra; Nehemiah; 1–2 Chronicles). In the following pages the prophetical books are presented in their chronological order so far as our knowledge allows. One advantage of this is in that it enables us better to locate the prophets historically, and also better to follow the development of their teaching.

# 29

# Joel

Keyword: visitation
Chapters: 3
Prophet No. 1
Southern Kingdom
Pre-Exilic
Pre-Assyrian Period
Date: 838–756 BC

*Joel* is the name of fourteen men mentioned in the Bible. It is compounded of two divine names, Yahveh (Jehovah) and El, and it means 'The Lord is God.'

The author of this book ministered either early or late in relation to the writing prophets. Both views are contended for. Recent scholarship is almost unanimous in assigning a post-exilic date, the fourth century, or later; but there are good reasons for the view that Joel was the earliest of the literary prophets, and ministered in the reign of Amaziah or Uzziah, that is, between 838–756 BC. The point of controversy is that he does not mention the Assyrians and Babylonians, and therefore must have written either before they became formidable, or after they had ceased to be so. If we accept the early date for this prophecy, Joel was contemporary with Jonah, Amos, and Hosea. In any case, his message is to Judah, and not to Israel.

The style is elegant, clear, and impassioned, and must be given a high place in Hebrew literature.

The book falls into two main parts. In the first, Joel speaks, and in the second, Jehovah. The first part is historical, and the second, prophetical. The first tells of desolation, and the second of deliverance.

The interpretation of the locusts may be actual, allegorical, or apocalyptical. Without doubt it is the first, and in all likelihood the other two also, the one pointing to an invasion of the land by hordes of enemies, and the other making the locusts emblems of world forces which shall appear in the last days.

The outstanding passages are those which relate to the locust invasion (2:1–11), the outpouring of the Holy Spirit (2:28–32; cf. Acts 2:16–21), and the final felicity of Judah (3:18–21).

Other things to note are: references to 'the Day of the Lord'; references to Tyre, Zidon, Palestine, Grecians, Sabeans, Egypt and Edom; and the message of 1:4 and 2:25.

# Analysis of Joel

## I. HISTORICAL – JOEL SPEAKS
Chapters 1:1–2:17
Key: Desolation

### 1. The Fact of Desolation (1:1–20)
Locusts Relentless in the Country
(i.)  The Situation                                                    1–4
        Hear (2). Tell (3). The Tale (4).

## II. PROPHETICAL – JEHOVAH SPEAKS
Chapters 2:18–3:21
Key: Deliverance

### 1. The Promise of Present Blessing (2:18–27)

### 2. The Promise of Future Blessing (2:28–3:21)

# 30

# Jonah

Keyword: commission
Chapters: 4
Prophet No. 2
Northern Kingdom
Pre-Exilic
Assyrian Period
Date: 840–784 BC

*Jonah*, which means 'dove', was a real person and not a creature of human fancy. The son of Amittai, of the tribe of Zebulun, he lived at Gathhepher, in the province of Zebulun, and was a prophet of the Northern Kingdom. We learn from 2 Kings 14:25 that he exercised his ministry during the reign of Jeroboam II (823–782 BC), and, it would seem, it was at his instigation that the coast of Israel was restored, and in his time the people attained to a height of prosperity which has no parallel in the history of this kingdom. Of himself and his work we know no more than this, and what is recorded in the book before us. His contemporaries were Joel, Amos, and Hosea.

This book is not really a prophecy, but the history of a prophet. With the exception of chapter 2, it is straightforward narrative, telling of Jonah's commission to Nineveh, and what he did with it.

Two opposite views are held of the historicity of the book. On the one hand it is regarded as 'an imaginative work with a moral lesson, and that the ancient prophet is chosen as its hero for his known anti-Assyrian bias'. On the other hand, it is regarded as genuinely historical, and it is claimed that Jesus believed it to be so (Mt. 12:39–41; 16:4; Lk. 11:29,30). In spite of all that has been said to the contrary, we take this latter view.

The object of the book seems to have been to correct the extreme form of Jewish nationalism which then prevailed, and to proclaim the mercy of God for Gentiles as well as for Jews. That the book may, and indeed, does, have an allegorical significance, we do not question. It is prophetic in outlook and catholic in spirit. Its subject is not a 'whale', but foreign missions. The book illustrates Faber's great lines,

> There's a wideness in God's mercy
> Like the wideness of the sea
> There's a kindness in His justice
> Which is more than liberty.

The miraculous element in it is only such as inheres in all Israel's history, authenticating the revelation which was given to them.

In Jonah, 'the religious spirit of the Old Testament reaches its purest and amplest expression.' Of it Charles Reade has said,

> Jonah is the most beautiful story ever written in so small a compass. It contains 48 verses and 1328 English words ... There is growth of character, a distinct plot worked

out without haste or crudity. Only a great artist could have hit on a perfect proportion between dialogue and narrative.

We agree that Jonah was 'a great artist', but do not believe that he 'hit on' the product of his genius, but rather that the Holy Spirit employed the ability He had given to him. Things to specially note are: the miraculous element in the story; the characterization of the heathen mariners (1:5–16); Jonah's prayer (2:1–9), trace its clauses in the psalms; what is said of Nineveh (3); Jonah's reason for fleeing (4:2); the number of young children in Nineveh (4:11); and the patience and mercy of God throughout.

## Analysis of Jonah

### I. THE DIVINE COMMISSION
Chapters 1:1–3:2

| | |
|---|---|
| 1. The First Call | 1:1–2 |
| 2. The Plight | 1:3 |
| 3. The Storm | 1:4–14 |
| 4. The Chastisement | 1:15–17 |
| 5. The Prayer | 2:1–10 |
| 6. The Second Call | 3:1–2 |

### II. THE NATIONAL CONSEQUENCE
Chapter 3:3–10

| | |
|---|---|
| 1. The Prophet's Message | 3,4 |
| 2. The Immediate Effect | 5,6 |
| 3. The Royal Edict | 7,8 |
| 4. The Heathen's Hope | 9 |
| 5. The Averted Judgment | 10 |

## III. THE PROPHET'S COMPLAINT
### Chapter 4

# 31

# Amos

Keyword: threatened
Chapters: 9
Prophet No. 3
Northern Kingdom
Pre-Exilic
Assyrian Period
Date: 810–785 BC

*Amos* means 'bearer' or 'borne' (by God), and he is the author of the book which bears his name (7:8; 8:1,2). If the date of Joel is late, and not early, as we have supposed, then, Amos began a new era of prophecy, in that he was the first to write his messages. According to the chronology adopted here, he was contemporary with Joel, Jonah, and Hosea. He tells us that he was a herdsman from the region of Tekoa, and while pursuing his daily round of duties he was, like Elisha, called to the high dignity of the prophetic ministry. He was not of the schools of the prophets, that is, he had no professional training, neither was he in the line of the prophets (7:14,15). His experience teaches us that God's agents are determined by the law of His choice, and not by any human succession or profession. His manner of life is reflected in the illustrations he employs, the bird in the nest, two men meeting in the desert, a shepherd snatching from the mouth of a lion two legs and the piece of an ear, sycamore trees, grasshoppers, a basket of summer fruit, the waggon loaded with sheaves, cattle-driving, corn-winnowing, and so on. But though Amos had no academic training, as we would say, it has been said that in vigour, vividness, and simplicity of speech he was not surpassed by any of his successors.

The book consists of a series of oracles (1:3–2:16), a series of sermons (3:1–6:14), and a series of visions (7:1–9:10), with an introduction and a conclusion. The style of Amos is elaborate and finished, and he is not limited to one literary form. The first part of his message is in the form of lyric prophecy (1–2), and here is a free interchange of rhythm and recitative, of poetry and prose. The poetic refrains tell of ideal transgressions and doom, and the prose portions tell of actual sins and sorrows. Mark the formula (1:3,4) which is eight times repeated. The second part of the message (3–6) is in the form of discourse, and here there are five speeches on the sin and doom of Israel. Each ends with a 'therefore', the first three beginning with 'Hear ye this word,' and the last two with 'Woe'. The third part (7–9) is in the form of dramatic vision, five visions, with narrative portions.

Amos charges Israel with avarice, injustice, un-cleanness, and profanity (2:6–12), and they excused themselves on the ground that they were the chosen people (3:2). The prophet's reply is that their relation to God is an aggravation of their offence. In the midst of Israel's compromise and corruption the prophet proclaims the sovereignty of God, the God of all creation (1:2; 4:13; 5:8).

The threats of doom are interspersed with exhortations to 'seek the Lord' (five times), and with the promise of a better day to dawn (9:11–15). Things to regard specially in this book are its style, figures of speech, autobiographical material, the political and religious situation at home and abroad, the story of Amaziah's opposition, and references to places and peoples.

# Analysis of Amos

## PROLOGUE (1:1)
The Prophet, and the Time of his Prophecy

## I. DECLARATION OF THE SIN AND JUDGMENT AGAINST EIGHT NATIONS (1:2–2:16)

1. Damascus (3)
2. Gaza (6)
3. Tyre (9)
4. Edom (11)
5. Ammon (13)
6. Moab (1)
7. Judah (4)
8. Israel (6)

## II. EXPANSION OF THE SIN AND JUDGMENT OF ISRAEL (chs. 3–6)

Discourse 1 – The Prophet is appointed to predict judgment (3).
Discourse 2 – The rejection of repeated warnings should lead them to prepare for judgment (4).
Discourse 3 – If they had sought the Lord, the 'Day of the Lord' would not have overtaken them, but now Assyria will usher in that Day (5–6).

### III. VISIONS OF THE SIN AND JUDGMENT OF ISRAEL (7–9:10)

1. The Devouring Locust. Prayer and Answer (7:1–3).
2. The Consuming Fire. Prayer and Answer (7:4–6).
3. The Searching Plumline. No Prayer and Answer (7:7–11,12–17). Historical Narrative.
4. The Basket of Summer Fruit. Judgment: its Consummation, Cause, and Character (8).
5. The Lord beside the Altar (9:1–10).

### EPILOGUE (9:11–15)

The Ultimate Restoration of Israel

# 32

# Hosea

Keyword: estrangement
Chapters: 14
Prophet No. 4
Northern Kingdom
Pre-Exilic
Assyrian Period
Date: 810–725 BC

Hosea, Hoshea, Joshua, and Jesus are identical in derivation, and mean 'salvation' (cf. Mt. 1:21). Hosea's contemporaries were Joel, Jonah, Amos, Isaiah, and Micah. As, in the South, Uzziah, Jotham, Ahaz, and Hezekiah reigned during his ministry, it would seem that he prophesied across a period of from sixty to seventy years, a longer time, probably, than any other prophet. He, too, ministered in the prosperous and corrupt reign of Jeroboam II. He is the first, but not the last, prophet whose personal history is made a symbol to his countrymen.

Unlike those of Amos, Hosea's language and style are difficult and abrupt. 'He flashes forth brilliant sentences, but writes no great chapters.' Here are not the imagination, the fire, and the vivid concreteness of Amos, but in some respects he is deeper; indeed, it has been said that his religious message is one of the most profound and spiritual in the Old Testament. The book falls into two main parts. The first part is personal (1–3), and the second is national (4–14). The faithless wife in the first division has her counterpart in the faithless people in the second; and the faithful husband in the one, answers to the faithful Lord in the other.

Hosea's *motif* is not common in literature. Much has been written of the loyalty of a pure woman to an unfaithful husband, but little of the loyalty of a strong man to an unfaithful wife. A comparison is found in Tennyson's treatment of Arthur's forgiveness of Guinevere,

> Lo! I forgive thee, as Eternal God
> Forgives: do thou for thine own soul the rest.

In the study of this book three things must be kept prominent.

First, the *personal narrative* (1–3), with its reference to the husband, the wife, and the children. Consider carefully the names of the children: Jezreel, 'God will scatter'; Lo-Ruhamah, 'Unpitied'; and Lo-Ammi, 'Not my People' (cf. I Pet. 2:10).

Second, the *national interpretation* (4–14), with its dominating notes: transgression, visitation, and restoration. Israel was situated midway between Egypt and Assyria, and in the kingdom two factions existed, one favouring alliance with the one Power, and the other, with the other power. Special reference to this is found in chapters 4:1–11:11. In Hosea are nine brief allusions to Judah, and no predictions concerning the Gentiles. The sins charged against the people are lying, perjury, drunkenness, lust, robbery, murder, treason, and regicide. The worship of Jehovah was corrupted with idolatry and profaned by formality.

Third, the *spiritual application* (1–14). If Amos emphasizes the 'severity' of God, Hosea emphasizes His 'goodness' (Rom. 11:22). There are passages here which, for pathos and love, are unrivalled (2:14,15,19,20; 3; 11:3,4,8; 14). This book emphasizes the shame of sin, the fruit of backsliding, the love of the Lord, and the conditions of restoration. Special chapters are the third and the fourteenth. In chapter 3 is a remarkable prophecy, verse 4, telling of the present, and verse 5, of the future of God's people, Israel. Chapter 14 is the greatest in the Bible for the backslider. Mark carefully the speakers in the several verses: Prophet, 1–3; Lord, 4–7; Ephraim, 8a; Lord, 8b; Ephraim, 8c; Lord, 8d; Prophet, 9.

The leading note of Hosea's utterances is an impassioned tenderness, in harmony with the personal experiences which he describes.

# Analysis of Hosea

## I. PERSONAL AFFLICTION (chs. 1–3)
The Faithless Wife and her Faithful Husband

### 1. The Children or Signs (1:1–2:1)
(i.)     First Sign: Gomer
(ii.)    Second Sign: Jezreel
(iii.)   Third Sign: Lo-ruhamah
(iv.)    Fourth Sign: Lo-ammi

## 2. The Wife or Backsliding (2:2–23)
(i.)     The Grievance of Love
(ii.)    The Severity of Love
(iii.)   The Goodness of Love

## 3. The Husband or Deliverance                    (3)
(i.)     Command                                      1
(ii.)    Obedience                                   2,3
(iii.)   Significance                                4,5

## I. NATIONAL REFLECTION (chs. 4–14)

The Faithless Nation and the Faithful Lord

### 1. The Transgression of Israel is Prominent (chs. 4–8)
Key: 2:1–5
(i.)     Idolatry
(ii.)    Anarchy

### 2. The Visitation of Israel is Prominent (9–11:11)
Key: 2:6–13
(i.)     Egypt–West
(ii.)    Assyria–East

### 3. The Restoration of Israel is Prominent (11:12–14)
Key: 2:14–23
(i.)     Retrospect
(ii.)    Prospect

# 33

# Isaiah

Keyword: salvation
Chapters: 66
Prophet No. 5
Southern Kingdom
Pre-Exilic
Assyrian Period
Date: 758–698 BC

The name *Isaiah* means 'Yahweh is salvation', or 'salvation of Yahweh'. The prophet received his call in the last year of the reign of Uzziah (756 BC), and continued until the time of Hezekiah, a period of not less than forty years. His contemporaries were Hosea and Micah. We are told that he was married (8:3), and had two, possibly three, sons (7:3, 8:1–4). The scene of his labours was chiefly, if not exclusively, Jerusalem. He is rightly called the evangelical prophet, and by common consent is one of the greatest of the prophets in splendour of intellectual endowments. He takes an unchallenged place among the very great writers whom humanity has produced. His power of vivid, luminous visualization of truth, touched with extraordinary depth of emotion is unmatched. He is equally distinguished for intensity and for majesty of utterance. The chapters of the second division of the book easily take their place in the very great literature of the world. Isaiah and Job are poets of superlative greatness.

The prophet stands midway between Moses and Christ, and begins to prophesy 217 years after the division of the United Kingdom. His ministry includes the last years of the Northern Kingdom.

The book falls into three distinct parts. The first is Prophetic (1–35); the second is Historic (36–39); and the third is Messianic (40–66). The keynote of the first part is, we may say, condemnation; of the second, confiscation, and of the third, consolation. In the first part Assyria is central; in the third part it is Babylon, and the second part points back to the one and forward to the other. Isaiah says that he and his children were for 'signs' (8:18), and this is very suggestive. Maher-shalal-hash-baz, means 'speed to the spoil, hurry to the prey', and represents chapters 1–39; Shear-jashub means 'a remnant shall return', and represents chapters 40–66; and Isaiah, which means 'salvation of the Lord', represents the whole book.

For about a century the Isaianic authorship of chapters 40–66, has been not only questioned, but denied, and such terms as 'the Deutero-Isaiah', 'the Babylonian Isaiah', and 'the Great Unnamed' have become commonplaces in this field of study. The question, as Professor A.B. Davidson has said 'is one of fact and criticism exclusively, and not a matter either of faith or practice'. It is most important to observe the different viewpoints of the two main divisions. In chapters 1–39, the prophet is addressing his own generation, but, if he wrote chapters 40–66, he is addressing a generation a century and a half after his time, the captives in

Babylon. If prediction be once admitted as an element in prophecy, the Spirit of God could well have used Isaiah to speak to a distant generation. The unity of the book has been learnedly argued, and certainly must not be airily dismissed.

What matters, of course, is the substance of this great book. In part one, mark specially the great indictment (ch. 1); the prophet's call and commission (ch. 6); the book of burdens (8–23), the book of songs (25–27); and the book of woes (28–32).

Part two (36–39) is very valuable for the light it throws on the character and time of Hezekiah. His Songs (38:20) are, in all likelihood, the songs of degrees, Psalms 120–134.

Part three (40–66) is one grand Messianic poem, the Rhapsody of Zion Redeemed, and is peerless literature. It is in three divisions of nine chapters each, and each division consists of three sections, and chapter 53 is the central chapter of the central section of the central division, and the central verses of this central chapter enshrine the central truth of the gospel (5, 6). These divisions and sections are:

A    (a) ch. 40; (b) 41; (c) 42:1–43:13;
      (a) 43:14–44:5; (b) 44:6–23; (c) 44:24–45:25;
      (a) 46; (b) 47; (c) 48.

B    (a) 49; (b) 50; (c) 51.
      (a) 52:1–12; (b) 52:13–53; (c) 54.
      (a) 55; (b) 56:1–8; (c) 56:9–57:21.

C    (a) 58; (b) 59; (c) 60;
      (a) 61; (b) 62; (c) 63:1–6.
      (a) 63:7–64:12; (b) 65; (c) 66.

The greatest chapters are the sixth and fifty-third.

# Analysis of Isaiah

## Division I—Prophetic (chs. 1–35)
### Keynote: Condemnation
### Outlook: Assyrian

## 1. Prophecies Concerning Judah and Israel (chs. 1–12)

| | | |
|---|---|---:|
| (i.) | The Great Indictment and Prediction of Judgment | 1–5 |
| (ii.) | The Prophet's Call and Commission | 6 |
| (iii.) | A Time Promised of Restoration and Thanksgiving | 7–12 |

## 2. Predictions Against Foreign Nations (chs. 13–23)

| | | |
|---|---|---:|
| (i.) | The Book of Burdens | |
| (ii.) | Philistia | 14:28–32 |
| (iii.) | Moab | 15–16 |
| (iv.) | Damascus | 18 |
| (v.) | Egypt | 13–20 |
| (vi.) | Babylon | 21:1–10 |
| (vii.) | Edom | 21:11–12 |
| (viii.) | Arabia | 21:13–17 |
| (ix.) | Jerusalem | 22 |
| (x.) | Tyre | 23 |

## 3. Announcements of Judgments and Deliverances (chs. 24–35)

| | | |
|---|---|---:|
| (i.) | A Picture of Universal Judgment | 24 |
| (ii.) | The Book of Songs | 25–27 |
| | (a) Song of the Oppressed Delivered | (25:1–8) |
| | (b) Song of the Enemy Humbled | (25:9–12) |
| | (c) Song in the Land of Judah | (26) |
| | (d) Song of the Restored Vineyard | (27) |
| (iii.) | The Book of Woes | 28–33 |
| | (a) Woe to the Crown of Pride | (28) |

### Division II – Historic (chs. 36–39)
Keynote: Confiscation
Outlook: Assyrian and Babylonian

### Division III–Messianic (chs. 40–66)
Keynote: Consolation
Outlook: Babylonian

## 1. The Deliverance (chs. 40–48)
God and the gods: Israel and the heathen compared.

## 2. The Deliverer (chs. 49–57)
The sufferings and the glory of Jehovah's servant compared.

## 3. The Delivered (chs. 58–66)
The faithful and the unfaithful, and their respective ends compared.

# 34

# Micah

Keyword: arraignment
Chapters: 7
Prophet No. 6
Northern and Southern Kingdoms
Pre-Exilic
Assyrian Period
Date: 750–695 BC

*Micah* is a combination of three Hebrew words which together mean 'who is like Yah!'.

*The Prophet and His Time*
Of the man himself we do not know much, but through the medium of his message we may judge of his personal qualities, and of his power as a preacher. His style is rapid, bold, and vivid. The introduction tells us that he ministered in the days of Jotham, Ahaz, and Hezekiah of the Southern Kingdom, and that means, during the reigns of Pekah and Hoshea of the Northern Kingdom. These reigns cover a period of fully sixty years, and these were years of political unrest and social decay. Micah is the only prophet whose ministry was directed

to both the areas, and the conditions in each gave shape to his message. His contemporaries were Hosea, a prophet in the north, and Isaiah, in the south, and he combined the dominant notes of each, with striking contrasts of detail and style.

## The Prophet and His Task

Isaiah's prophetism had in it a political element; he was concerned on account of the attempt of Israel and Syria to force Judah into an alliance with them against Assyria; but Micah has nothing to say about this. Isaiah was a prophet of the court and city, but Micah was a country prophet. He was much occupied with the moral and social condition of the people, and of this he writes graphically. No class was exempt from the prevailing corrupting influences: princes, priests, prophets, and people were all victims of social disorder and moral decay (2:2,8,9,11; 3:1–3,5,11). Micah shows that, notwithstanding this state of things, they clung to religious ordinances and spiritual forms, and he exposes the futility of this (6:7,8).

## The Prophet and His Testimony

It was no easy task which Micah had, but he brought to it strong qualities and a great belief in God and righteousness. He tears aside the veil which hid their sin and shame from view, and he denounces their iniquities in scathing terms. In short sharp sentences he brings his whip down upon the venal judges, the corrupt priests, and the hireling prophets, and makes them smart beneath the lash. He tells them also of coming judgment (3:12; 4:10; 6:16). But, like his prophet brothers, he looks beyond, to a time of restoration. In the storm he sang a song; in the night he caught a glimpse of the morning. With his threats are mingled promises (4:1–8 cf. 1:9–16; 5:7,8; 3:6,7,12; with 2:12; 4:10; 5:8,6).

The classic passage in this book is 6:8; of which Huxley wrote,

> In the eighth century before Christ, in the heart of a world of idolatrous polytheists, the Hebrew prophet put forth a conception of religion which appears to me as wonderful an inspiration of genius as the art of Phidias, or the science of Aristotle. If any so-called religion takes away from this great saying of Micah, I think it wantonly mutilates; while if it adds thereto, I think it obscures the perfect ideal of religion.

## Analysis of Micah

### I. THE PEOPLE SUMMONED TO ATTEND
### (chs. 1–2)
'Hear, all ye people' (1:2)

| | | |
|---|---|---|
| 1. | A Declaration of Impending Judgment | 1:2–16 |
| 2. | A Rehearsal of the Reasons for this Judgment | 2:1–11 |
| 3. | A Promise of Blessing Beyond the Judgment | 2:12,13 |

### II. THE LEADERS SUMMONED TO ATTEND
### (chs. 3–5)
'Hear, O heads of Jacob' (3:1)

| | | |
|---|---|---|
| 1. | The Sin of the Leaders, and the Consequence | 3 |
| 2. | A Promise of Restoration and Blessing | 4:1–8 |
| 3. | Israel's sure Travail, but ultimate Triumph | 4:9–5:15 |

# III. THE MOUNTAINS SUMMONED TO ATTEND
## (chs. 6–7)
### 'Hear ye, O mountains' (6:1–9)

# 35

# Nahum

Keyword: doom
Chapters: 3
Prophet No. 7
Southern Kingdom
Pre-Exilic
Assyrian Period
Date: 663–606 BC

*Nahum*, which means 'compassion', or 'consolation', directs his message against Nineveh. About 130 years before, Jonah had delivered a message there, and with what results we know (Jon. 3:5–10). Now, the doom of the city is proclaimed. The dates between which Nahum predicted are 663 BC, when Thebes fell (3:8–10), and 606 BC, when Nineveh fell; in all likelihood this prophecy belongs to the year 650 BC, or there about.

As to its literary form, Professor R. Moulton says that the prophecy 'hovers between the doom song and the rhapsodic discourse'; and as to its quality, De Wette observes that, 'It is a classic in all respects. It is marked by clearness, by its finished elegance, as well as by fire, richness, and originality. The rhythm is regular and lively.' How brilliant and spirited is his description of a battle (3:2,3). Two things characterise the prophecy; first, the prophet does not allude to the sin of his people, nor to any impending wrath to be visited upon them (cf. 1:12,13,15); and second, his gaze is fixed upon the enemies of Judah. At the time of this pronouncement Nineveh appeared to be impregnable, with walls 100 feet high, and broad enough for three chariots to drive abreast on them; with a circumference of 60 miles, and adorned by more than 1200 towers. But what are bricks and mortar to God! The mighty empire which Tiglath-Pileser, Shalmaneser, Sargon, Sennacherib, Esarhaddon, and Asshur-banipal had built up, the Lord threw down at a stroke, and that beyond all recovery. In the second century after Christ, not a vestige of it remained, and its very site was long a matter of uncertainty.

This is a prophecy of doom, and we may not look here for the spiritual element which we find in Hosea, Micah, and Isaiah, though the majesty and mercy of God in 1:1–8, should be carefully studied.

It is a book which should bring much comfort in these days to all lovers of righteousness. In our time, as then, proud civilizations, so-called, are staking everything upon the strength of their fighting power on land and sea and in the air, and their boast, as we might expect, is characterized by a monstrous disregard of God, His righteousness and sovereignty; but again, as long ago, men and nations will have to learn that God is on the throne, and that, 'His Kingdom ruleth over all.'

# Analysis of Nahum

## I. JUDGMENT UPON NINEVEH DECLARED
### (ch. 1)

1. The Character and Power of the Lord  1–8
2. The Destruction of Nineveh, and the
   Peace of Judah  9–15

## II. JUDGMENT UPON NINEVEH DESCRIBED
### (ch. 2)

1. The Siege and Capture of the City  1–8
2. The Utter Sack of the City  9–13

## III. JUDGMENT UPON NINEVEH DEFENDED
### (ch. 3)

1. Because of her sin she shall be overthrown 1–7
2. Her great wealth and strength cannot
   suffice to save her  8–19

# 36

# Zephaniah

Keyword: vindication
Chapters: 3
Prophet No. 8
Southern Kingdom
Pre-Exilic
Assyrian Period
Date: 630–610 BC

*Zephaniah* means 'he whom Jehovah hides', or 'Jehovah is hidden.' The prophet was, most probably, the great-great-grandson of Hezekiah, and he prophesied in the early years of Josiah's reign, and his words promoted, no doubt, the revival which took place in the eighteenth year of that king's rule. Zephaniah ministered between Nahum and Jeremiah; was contemporary with the former, and, possibly, with the latter also. This prophecy reflects the dark days which followed the reigns of Manasseh and Amon. It follows the main prophetic line, denouncing sin, pronouncing judgment, and announcing restoration. These predictions refer not only to the chosen people, but also to the nations, as in Isaiah and Ezekiel. The whole earth is the theatre where the divine Judge displays the grandeur of His law and the glory of His love.

The dominating note of this book is 'The Day of the Lord', an expression which, in all the prophetic books, points to a time of judgment.

From a literary point of view, Zephaniah is much inferior to Nahum, yet, its descriptions are vivid. Two contrasted passages are worthy of special attention, namely, 1:14–18, describing judgment, and 3:14–17, describing blessing.

# Analysis of Zephaniah

## I. A DECLARATION OF RETRIBUTION (ch. 1)
### Introduction (1)

## 1. The Scope of Judgment (2,3)

## 2. The Cause of Judgment (4–6)
| | | |
|---|---|---|
| (i.) | Idolatry | 4,5a |
| (ii.) | Oscillation | 5b |
| (iii.) | Apostasy | 6 |

## 3. The Subjects of Judgment (7–13)
| | | |
|---|---|---|
| (i.) | Princes | 8 |
| (ii.) | Oppressors | 9,10 |
| (iii.) | Merchants | 11 |
| (iv.) | The Indifferent | 12,13 |

## 4. The Nature of Judgment (14–18)

# II. AN EXHORTATION TO REPENTANCE
## (2:1–3:8a)

## 1. The Call to Judah (2:1–3)

## 3. The Sin of Jerusalem (3:1–5)

## 4. The Fate of the Obdurate (3:6–8a)

# III. A PROMISE OF REDEMPTION (3:8b–20)

## 1. The Conversion of the Nations (8b–10)

## 2. The Restoration of Israel (11–13)

## 3. The Day of Jubilation (14–17)

## 4. The Reproach Rolled Away (18–20)

# 37

# Jeremiah

Keyword: warning
Chapters: 52
Prophet No. 9
Southern Kingdom
Pre-Exilic and Exilic
Assyrian and Babylonian Periods
Date : 627–585 BC

*Jeremiah* seems to mean 'whom Yah casts or appoints'. This book is of immense importance, on autobiographical, historical, and prophetical grounds, but all we can do within our present limits is to suggest how the study of it may be approached.

*The Time of Jeremiah*
In the prophetic office he was preceded by Joel, Jonah, Amos, Hosea, Isaiah, Micah, and Nahum; and he was contemporary with Zephaniah, Habakkuk, and Obadiah in the land, and, for a time, with Ezekiel and Daniel in the east. He saw five kings upon the throne of Judah: Josiah, Jehoahaz, Jehoiakim, Jehoiachin, and Zedekiah; and he was to Josiah what Isaiah had been

to Hezekiah. Five years after Jeremiah's call the Book
of the Law was found in the Temple (2 Kings 22), the
reading of which led to widespread confession and
apparent reformation, but the work was not deep, and
with the death of Josiah, Judah's last hope passed away.
The condition of things is reflected in chapters 10–12;
and it was at such a time as this that the prophet was
called to his thankless but necessary task.

## The Person of Jeremiah

This book has been called 'a prophetic autobiography'
for, in these pages, the prophet himself stands revealed;
timid, sensitive, sympathetic, loyal, courageous, plain-
tive, retiring, tender, severe, and patient. None of the
other prophets comes so near to us in a human way as
Jeremiah, and as a sufferer perhaps no other character
comes so near to this man of sorrows.

## The Task of Jeremiah

He was told at the beginning what he had to do and
what he might expect, and he was promised divine
support (1:10–19). He had in a decadent age and to a
stiff-necked people to proclaim unwelcome truth, and
he had his full share of the consequences that generally
accompany such a task.

His message passed through certain well-defined
stages. There is first the note of denunciation. Jehovah
had delivered this people from Egyptian bondage, had
led them through the wilderness, and had wonderfully
revealed Himself to them, and His will for them, but
they had forsaken Him, they had walked after vanity
and become vain. Following on this is the note of
visitation. Sin must be punished; with evil comes its
inevitable and just reward (16:9,13; 25:11).

But these people were 'the dearly beloved of Jehovah's soul' (21:7), and so there is added the note of invitation. While there is life there is hope; upon repentance will come blessing. God is both just and gracious; and so the people are called upon to amend their ways (7:3; 18:7–11).

One other note is struck, the note of consolation. Beyond rebellion will be repentance, and glory will follow the gloom (30–33). During the storm a vision is caught of coming calm, the dawning of a better day. These predictions include the restoration from Babylonian captivity, but they go beyond that, to the time of Christ's next Advent and the final recovery of Israel.

## *The Book of Jeremiah*

Much ingenuity has been spent in the endeavour to place chronologically the various utterances of this prophet, but finality in this need not be expected. It is clear that his messages are not in chronological order in his book, but seem to be presented according to some group scheme. It is useful, however, for us to re-arrange the material so that we may follow the historical course of events.

The ministry of Jeremiah falls into three main divisions, separated by long silences, and corresponding to the reigns of the three chief kings under whom he prophesied. The first period was under Josiah, and was mainly one of appeal, enforced by declaration of coming visitation. The second period was under Jehoiakim, and was one of warning, deepening into irrevocable judgment. The third period was under Zedekiah, and was one of reconstruction, seeking to establish a new order amid the ruins of the old. These three periods cover forty-five years; the first, twenty years, 628–608

BC; the second, eleven years, 608–597 BC, and the third, fourteen years, 597–583 BC. The substance of Jeremiah's messages in these periods is indicated in the following analysis.

## The Interest of Jeremiah

This book surpasses all others in the Bible in its intensely human interest. There is a biographical interest: the characters of the period – Jeremiah, Baruch, Josiah, Jehoiakim, Zedekiah, Necho, Nebuchadnezzar. There is a historical interest: the stirring events of the period – finding the Book of the Law, the reformation, battles of Megiddo and Carchemish, Nebuchadnezzar's invasion of Judah, Jeremiah's Rolls and Jehoiakim's vandalism, and the destruction of Jerusalem. There is a prophetical interest – the seventy years' captivity, the future of Babylon and of Israel. There is a doctrinal interest – Jeremiah's teaching on God, the kingdom, sin, repentance, judgment, the Messiah, the new covenant, personal responsibility, redemption, destiny. This is a book to be known and loved.

# Analysis of Jeremiah
(Chronologically Arranged)

## Introduction: Chapter 1
## The Prophet's Call And Commission

## I. PROPHECIES BEFORE THE FALL OF JERUSALEM

### 1. Prophecies in the Reign of Josiah

(i.)    First Movement                                          2–6
        Judah's Sin; A Call to Repentance;
        Prediction of Judgment

(ii.)  Second Movement                              7–9
       Indictments, Threatenings, the Prophet's
       Grief, and Wailing called for
(iii.) Third Movement                               10–12
       Idolatry, Disobedience, Treachery, The
       Lord's Disappointment with His People

## 2. Prophecies in the Reign of Jehoiakim

(i.)   Order. Chs. 26; 46–49:33; 25; 36:1–8; 45; 36:9–32;
       14–15; 16; 17; 18–19:13; 19:14–20; 35; 22–23:8;
       23:9–40; 13.
(ii.)  Substance. Jeremiah predicts judgment
       against the nations and Judah; reproves false
       prophets; foretells the Babylonian invasion; and
       suffers for his message.

## 3. Prophecies in the Reign of Zedekiah

(i.)   Order. Chs. 24; 27; 28–29; 49:34–51; 21; 34;
       37–38; 39:15–18; 32; 33; 30; 31; 39:1–14.
(ii.)  Substance. Great Prediction against Babylon;
       Jeremiah's imprisonment; Prophecies of
       restoration; Jerusalem taken and Zedekiah's
       fate.

## II. PROPHECIES AFTER THE FALL OF JERUSALEM

## 1. The Remnant in Judah                          40–43:3

## 2. The Remnant in Egypt                          43:4–44

Conclusion: Chapter 52
Historical supplement.

# 38

# Habakkuk

Keyword: justice
Chapters: 3
Prophet No. 10
Southern Kingdom
Pre-Exilic
Babylonian Period
Date: 608–598 BC

*Habakkuk*, which means 'embracing', was contemporary with Jeremiah at home, and with Daniel abroad; and he prophesied, almost certainly, in the reigns of Jehoahaz and Jehoiakim. The state of things recorded in chapter 1:2–4, reflects the conditions in Jehoiakim's time, and the threatened invasion of the Chaldeans ties in with the facts recorded in 2 Kings 24–25.

The literary form of the prophecy is unique among the prophetic books. The prophet casts his thought into a dramatic representation, with Jehovah and himself as the speaker. His first complaint is because of the apostasy of Judah, and his second is that the Lord could and would use as the instrument of chastisement such a wicked people as the Chaldeans. The divine reply to the latter complaint is the heart of the book (2:4). It announces the divine principle of righteousness which, in effect, is 'The unjust shall die: the just shall live.' This principle is applied, first to the Chaldeans (2:5–20), and then to Judah (ch. 3). In the first application a fivefold 'woe' is pronounced against the Chaldeans, and the second application is a sublime theophany and its effect. The text of the effect (3:16–19) is one of the finest things in the Bible.

The central thought of the prophecy is quoted three times in the New Testament, but with varying emphasis. In Romans 1:17, the emphasis is on 'just'; in Galatians 3:11, it is on 'faith'; and in Hebrews 10:38 it is on 'live'.

The theophanic ode (ch. 3) was set to music and sung at public worship by the Jews.

## Analysis of Habakkuk

### I. THE COMPLAINT (1:1–11)

### 1. The Indictment against Judah (2–4)

### 2. The Invasion of the Chaldeans (5–11)

### II. THE APPEAL (1:12–2:20)

### 1. The Remonstrance (1:12–2:1)
| | | |
|---|---|---|
| (i.) | The Challenge | 1:12–14 |
| (ii.) | The Charge | 1:15,16 |
| (iii.) | The Conclusion | 1:17–2:1 |

**2. The Reply (2:2–20)**

## III. THE SONG (ch. 3)

**1. The Cry for Revival (2)**

**2. The Vision of Jehovah (3–15)**

**3. The Effect on the Prophet (16–19)**

# 39

# Daniel

Keyword: dominion
Chapters: 12
Prophet No. 11
God's Universal Kingdom
Exilic
Babylonian and Medo-Persian Periods
Date: 606–534 BC

*Daniel*, which means 'God is my Judge', spoke and wrote in exile, as did Ezekiel and John. He, with others, was deported from Judah in 606 BC, being then about twenty years of age, and three years later his recorded ministry began. As this ministry continued into the Persian period, Daniel must have been over ninety years of age at his death. His contemporaries were Jeremiah, Habakkuk, Ezekiel, and Obadiah.

This book is not among the prophets in the Hebrew Bible, but is one of the five 'Latter Writings' (Kethubim), the others being Ezra, Nehemiah, 1 and 2 Chronicles. In its contents the book is historical, prophetical, and apocalyptical. About half of it is history, and about half is prophetic-apocalypse. The first half is narration, and the second half is revelation. It was written for the Jews in captivity, and for generations unborn. The subject is the future trends and end of 'the times of the Gentiles' (Lk. 21:24), and the universal kingdom of God's appointed King. The focus of the book is 'the time of the end' (2:28,29,45; 8:17,19,23, et al.). The period covered is 72 years. In chs. 1–6, Daniel is spoken of, third person; and in chs. 7–12, Daniel speaks, first person.

The chronological order of the chapters is, with their dates: 1 (606), 2 (603), 3 (?), 4 (?), 7 (541), 8 (538), 5 (538), 9 (537), 6 (537), 10 (533), 11 (533), 12 (533). Chapters 2:4–7:28, are in Aramaic, and 1:1–2:3, 8–12, are in Hebrew.

The book of Daniel is a prophetic philosophy of history, and is the greatest book in the Bible on godless kingdoms and the kingdom of God. These are portrayed in chapter 2, from the human standpoint, by a dream; and in chapter 7, from the divine standpoint, by visions. In the one view the world's kingdoms are likened to a powerful Colossus, and in the other view, to four vicious beasts.

In addition to these two great revelations are the vision of the two beasts in chapter 7, the prophecy of the seventy-sevens in chapter 9, and the unveiling of the scripture of truth in chapters 11:1–12:4.

The two heathen monarchs of the book are Nebuchadnezzar and Belshazzar. The empires introduced are the Babylonian, Medo-Persian, Grecian, and Roman. The portrait of Daniel himself is one of the values of the book, and his prayer in chapter 11 is one of its great passages.

# Analysis of Daniel

## I. HISTORICAL (chs. 1–6)

### 1. The Reign of Nebuchadnezzar (chs. 1–4)
| | | |
|---|---|---|
| (i.) | The King's Food and the Faithful Jews | 1 |
| (ii.) | Vision of the Image and its Meaning | 2 |
| (iii.) | The Golden God and the Faithful Jews | 3 |
| (iv.) | Vision of the Tree and its Meaning | 4 |

### 2. The Reign of Belshazzar (ch. 5)
| | | |
|---|---|---|
| (i.) | The Feast and the Handwriting | 1–6 |
| (ii.) | The Interpretation and the Fulfilment | 7–31 |

### 3. The Reign of Darius (ch. 6)
| | | |
|---|---|---|
| (i.) | Daniel's Office and his Danger | 1–15 |
| (ii.) | Daniel's Deliverance and his God | 16–28 |

## II. PROPHETICAL (chs. 7–12)

### 1. The Reign of Belshazzar (chs. 7, 8)
| | | |
|---|---|---|
| (i.) | The Vision of the Four Beasts and its Meaning | 7 |
| (ii.) | The Vision of the Two Beasts and its Meaning | 8 |

### 2. The Reign of Darius (ch. 9)
| | | |
|---|---|---|
| (i.) | Daniel's Supplication | 1–19 |
| (ii.) | Gabriel's Revelation | 20–27 |

### 3. The Reign of Cyrus (chs. 10–12)
| | | |
|---|---|---|
| (i.) | Vision by the Hiddekel | 10 |
| (ii.) | Prophecies concerning Persia and Grecia | 11:1–33 |
| (iii.) | Prophecies concerning 'the time of the end' | 11:34–12:3 |
| (iv.) | Daniel, and the final Word | 12:4–13 |

# 40

# Ezekiel

Keyword: glory
Chapters: 48
Prophet No. 12
Exilic
Babylonian Period
Date: 592–572 BC

*Ezekiel*, which means 'God strengthens', was taken into Babylonian captivity with Jehoiachim in 599 BC, being about twenty-three years of age, and seven years later he began his prophetic ministry and continued for twenty years. Like Jeremiah, he was a priest as well as a prophet. Of the three major prophets, Isaiah was the great poet, Jeremiah was the great preacher, and Ezekiel was the great artist. Isaiah had blown the silver trumpet over Jerusalem, Jeremiah was playing the mournful flute in Judah, and Ezekiel was striking the iron harp by the Chebar. This prophet has not the sustained flight of Isaiah, nor the tenderness or Jeremiah, but there is a directness, which is common only to stern strong natures.

The style and method of Ezekiel are unique. Symbolic action often supplies the text for his message, as in the mimic siege of Jerusalem (ch. 4).

In addition to this emblem prophecy, are visions, as in ch. 8; similitudes, as in ch. 16; parables, as in ch. 17; poems, as in ch. 19; proverbs, as in ch. 12:22,23; 18:2; allegories, as in chs. 16, 23; and prophecies, as in chs. 6, 20, 40–48. No artist has given us pictures so inspiring, so mysterious, so charming and so terrifying as these.

The dominating notes of his ministry are sin, punishment, repentance, and blessing. To destroy false hopes and to awaken true ones was the burden of his soul.

The book falls into three distinct parts:

1.  Predictions *before* the Siege of Jerusalem: chs. 1–24; 592–588 BC; 4½ years.
2.  Predictions *during* the Siege of Jerusalem: chs. 25–32; 588–586 BC; 2 years.
3.  Predictions *after* the Siege of Jerusalem: chs. 33–47, 586–572 BC; 14 years.

The subjects treated in these parts are, the denunciation of Judah; the visitation of the nations; and the restoration of Israel.

The book begins with heavenly glory, in the cherubic vision (ch. 1); it ends with earthly glory, in the vision of the new order (chs. 40–48); and in between, it tells of the departing glory (8:4; 9:3; 10:4,18,19; 11:22,23). The idea of glory runs through the whole prophecy, and, in a sense, characterises it.

Ezekiel has been called 'the prophet of reconstruction' and this he was. He saw a great future not for Judah only, but for the whole nation, when it shall have been reunited and purified (chs. 36–37). With Jeremiah, he shares in the distinction of promulgating the doctrine of individual responsibility, but he gives it an emphasis, which is all its own (cf. Jer. 31:29,30; Ezek. 18).

# Analysis of Ezekiel

### I. DENUNCIATION OF JUDAH (chs. 1–24)
Predictions before the Siege of Jerusalem
4½ years    592–588 BC

### 1. The Prophet's Call and Commission (chs. 1–3)
| | | |
|---|---|---|
| (i.) | The Vision | 1:1–28 |
| (ii.) | The Voice | 2–3 |

### 2. Prophecies of Approaching Judgment (chs. 4–7)
| | | |
|---|---|---|
| (i.) | Symbolically Presented | 4, 5 |
| (ii.) | Plainly Predicted | 6, 7 |

### 3. The Moral Necessity for Judgment (chs. 8–11)
| | | |
|---|---|---|
| (i.) | Judah's Guilt and Punishment | 8, 9 |
| (ii.) | The Vision of the Cherubim | 10 |
| (iii.) | The Sin of the Princes and Hope of the Penitent | 11 |

### 4. The Absolute Certainty of Judgment (chs. 12–19)
| | | |
|---|---|---|
| (i.) | The Captivity Foretold, and the Leaders Rebuked | 12–14 |
| (ii.) | Judah, Fruitless and Faithless, Exposed | 15, 16 |
| (iii.) | The Overthrow Described, Deserved, and Lamented | 17–19 |

### 5. The Character of Judah the Cause of Judgment (chs. 20–24)
| | | |
|---|---|---|
| (i.) | Jehovah's Goodness and Judah's Guilt | 20:1–44 |

## II. VISITATION OF THE NATIONS (chs. 25–32)
Predictions *during* the Siege of Jerusalem
2 years   588–586 BC

## III. RESTORATION OF ISRAEL (chs. 33–48)
Predictions *after* the Siege of Jerusalem
14 years   586–572 BC

### 1. Predictions of New Life to be Bestowed (chs. 33–39)

### 2. Descriptions of the New Order to be Established (chs. 40–48)

# 41

# Obadiah

Keyword: retribution
Chapter: 1
Prophet No. 13
Exilic
Babylonian Period
Date: 586–585 BC

*Obadiah*, which means 'servant of Jehovah', received this 'vision' about the time of Judah's overthrow in 586. Of the prophet we know nothing, and although his message is short it is significant. His contemporary was Jeremiah. His word is against Edom, as Nahum's was against Nineveh. The Edomites were the posterity of Esau, and consistently were Israel's enemies. The quarrel between the two brothers was reflected in their posterity. When Jerusalem fell, the Edomites rejoiced (cf. Lam. 4:21,22; Psa. 87:7).

The overthrow of this people, it is said, is certain (1–9). They will be unseated from their security (3,4), plundered by enemies (5,6), deserted by allies (7), and stripped of wisdom and might (8,9). The reason for this is given (10–14); namely, for her bitter hostility to

Jacob her brother (10), for her shameful alliance with Judah's foes (11), and for the part she played at the time of Judah's overthrow (12–14). In consequence of this, Edom will be overthrown; her punishment will be retributive (15,16).

On the other hand, Israel will be delivered, and 'possess their possessions' (17–21). Some think that the prophet speaks here, not of the calamity in 586 BC, but of the capture and plunder of Jerusalem by the Philistines and Arabians in 848–844 BC. Obadiah's message is a rebuke of pride and unbrotherliness, and an affirmation of the law of retribution (cf. Jer. 49; Ezek. 25).

In form the prophecy is lyric exultation with divine monologue.

## Analysis of Obadiah

### I. THE DOOM OF EDOM (1–16)

| | |
|---|---:|
| 1. The Certainty of the Overthrow | 1–9 |
| 2. The Reason for the Overthrow | 10–14 |
| 3. The Character of the Overthrow | 15,16 |

### II. THE DELIVERANCE OF ISRAEL (17–21)

| | |
|---|---:|
| 1. The Triumph of Israel | 17,18 |
| 2. The Possessions of Israel | 19,20 |
| 3. The Establishment of Israel | 21 |

# 42

# Haggai

Keyword: consider
Chapters: 2
Prophet No. 14
To the Jews
Post-Exilic
Medo-Persian Period
Date: 520 BC

At this point we enter upon a new prophetic period. The history of the people of Israel, as to government, is divisible into three periods:

(1) Israel under judges, Moses to Samuel;
(2) Under kings, Saul to Zedekiah;
(3) Under priests, Joshua to the destruction of Jerusalem in 70 AD.

Viewed in relation to the captivity, the periods are: (1) Pre-Exilic; (2) Exilic; and (3) Post-Exilic. Or, viewed in relation to the world empires, the periods are: (1) the Assyrian; (2) the Babylonian; and (3) the Medo-Persian. Haggai, Zechariah, and Malachi ministered in the third of each of these periods.

*Haggai*, which means 'festal', and who prophesied in 520 BC, was, no doubt, born in captivity, and returned to the land under Zerubbabel. The foundation of the Temple had been laid, but the work had for long been at a standstill, and it was to urge the people to complete it that Haggai prophesied. His ministry lasted for about four months, during which time he delivered four messages on four different dates.

> Sixth month – first day – 1:2–11
> Seventh month – twenty-first day – 2:1–9
> Ninth month – twenty-fourth day – 2:10–19
> Ninth month – twenty-fourth day – 2:20–23

The message of the book to us is: do the duty, which lies to hand, with unwavering faith and steady perseverance, in spite of opposition. 'Be strong and work.'

## Analysis of Haggai

### I. THE WORD OF REPROOF (ch. 1)

| | |
|---|---|
| 1. The Temple of the Lord is Unfinished | 1–6 |
| 2. The Trouble of the People is Explained | 7–11 |
| 3. The Testimony of the Prophet is Heeded | 12–15 |

### II. THE WORD OF SUPPORT (2:1–9)

| | |
|---|---|
| 1. The Depression of the People | 1–3 |
| 2. The Promise of the Lord | 4,5 |
| 3. The Glory of the Temple | 6–9 |

## III. THE WORD OF BLESSING (2:10–19)

## IV. THE WORD OF PROMISE (2:20–23)

# 43

# Zechariah

Keyword: consummation
Chapters: 14
Prophet No. 15
To the Jews
Post-exilic
Medo-Persian Period
Date: 520–518 BC

*Zechariah*, which means 'one whom Jehovah remembers', was contemporary with Haggai, was his junior in years (2:4), and spoke for the same purpose. He, too, no doubt, was born in captivity, and returned under Zerubbabel. He and Haggai both prophesied in the second year of Darius Hystaspes, and their ministries were eminently effective.

The prophecy falls into two main divisions, chs. 1–7 and 9–14; and each of these is in two parts. The authorship of chs. 11–14 is uncertain, and in Matthew 27:9,10, a quotation from this division is attributed to Jeremiah. The style differs from that of chs. 1–8; the circumstances are wholly changed; visions have ceased, and prophecy rises to a more solemn strain.

The following analysis indicates the subject of the four parts.

Zechariah saw eight visions in one eventful night: the angelic horsemen (1:7–17); the four horns and the four smiths (1:18–21); the man with the measuring line (2); Joshua the high priest (3); the candlestick and the olive trees (4); the flying roll (5:1–4); the ephah and the woman (5:5–11); and the four chariots and horses (6:1–8).

The symbolic act which follows (6:9–15), is designed to show that the promised branch will exercise, as did Melchisedec, the double office of priest-king, when he returns to the earth to set up his millennial kingdom. In chs. 7–8, in reply to an inquiry as to whether certain fasts were now to be observed (7:1–3), a fourfold answer is given: (1) They should discover their motive in fasting, and remember the former years (7:4–7); (2) the Lord requires inward righteousness rather than outward forms (7:8–14); (3) the Lord will restore to his people what they had lost (8:1–7); and (4) the fasts will be turned into feasts of gladness (8:8–23).

In division two (chs. 9–14) are two burdens (9:1; 12:1). The first burden is to the effect that Israel will be reunited and restored; and the second is to the effect that before this restoration there will be judgment on Israel because of their rejection of the Messiah; but all their enemies will be overthrown, and they at last shall be characterised by 'holiness unto the Lord'.

Three great ideas characterise this book, namely, a universal purpose, a Messianic hope, and divine sovereignty.

# Analysis of Zechariah

## I. THE CHOSEN PEOPLE AND THE TEMPLE
### Chapters 1–8

### 1. The Visions of the Seer (chs. 1–6)
| | | |
|---|---|---|
| (i.) | A Warning Word | 1:1–6 |
| (ii.) | A Series of Visions | 1:7–6:8 |
| (iii.) | A Symbolic Act | 6:9–15 |

### 2. The Fasts and the Feasts (chs. 7, 8)
| | | |
|---|---|---|
| (i.) | An Urgent Inquiry concerning Fasts | 7: 1–3 |
| (ii.) | A Fourfold Answer introducing Feasts | 7:4–8 |

## II. THE MESSIANIC KING AND THE KINGDOM
### Chapters 9–14

*First Burden*
### 1. The Final Restoration of Judah and Israel (chs. 9–11)
| | | |
|---|---|---|
| (i.) | The Destruction of the Enemy | 9:1–8 |
| (ii.) | The Restoration of the People | 9:9–10 |
| (iii.) | The Rejection of the Shepherd | 11 |

*Second Burden*
### 2. The World-Drama of Judgment and Redemption (chs. 12–14)
| | | |
|---|---|---|
| (i.) | The Messianic Forecast | 12–13:6 |
| (ii.) | The Messianic Method | 13:7–14:15 |
| (iii.) | The Messianic Triumph | 14:16–21 |

# 44

# Malachi

Keyword: apostasy
Chapters: 4
Prophet No. 16
To the Jews
Post-Exilic
Medo-Persian Period
Date: 433–397 BC

*Malachi* means 'my messenger', and whether it is the name of the author of this book, or a title employed to express his mission, is not certain (cf. 3:1). This is the last of the Old Testament prophecies. The setting of it is in the stirring time of Nehemiah, and Malachi was to that reformer what Haggai and Zechariah had been to Zerubbabel. Following on a period of religious revival (Neh. 10:28–39), the people became religiously indifferent and morally lax, and it is this state of things, which Malachi rebukes (cf. Neh. 13:4–31).

The attitude of the people is exhibited in the sevenfold 'wherein' (1:2,6,7; 2:17; 3:7,8,13), and the charge which Malachi brought against them is fourfold, relating to things religious, moral, social, and material. Religiously, they were guilty of profanity and sacrilege; morally, of sorcery, adultery, perjury, fraud, and oppression; socially, they were untrue to their family responsibilities; and materially, they were 'robbing God' of the tithes due to him.

The prophecy ends with a reference backward to Moses, and forward to Elijah, that is, John the Baptist. The heart of hope in the prophecy is the verses 3:10,16–18.

Malachi's message is eminently necessary and appropriate today, for these abuses have their equivalents in the modern church. How prevalent is 'a form of godliness', the power being denied; how weak are many Christians with regard to great moral questions; how frequent is alliance in marriage of saved and unsaved; and how shamefully lax are Christians in the matter of giving their wealth and energies to God's work. To this situation Malachi still speaks.

At the end of the first book of the Old Testament we read of a 'coffin', and at the end of the last book we read of a 'curse', indicating that, till then, all was failure; but the Second Man, the Lord from glory, having come, the New Testament opens and closes in better terms; grace triumphant at last.

# Analysis of Malachi

## I. RELIGIOUS DECLENSION (1–2:9)

1. Expression of Jehovah's love for Israel          1:1–5
2. Expostulation with the Priests for their offences                                          1:6–14
3. Execration of the Priests for their indifference 2:1–9

## II. SOCIAL DEBASEMENT (2:10–16)

Condemnation of the Priests and the People
 (a) For Alien Marriages
 (b) For Cruel Divorces

## III. MORAL DEFLECTION (2:17–4:6)

1. The coming of the Lord for Judgment   2:17–3:6
2. The charge preferred against the People   3:7–12
3. The contrast between the righteous and the wicked   3:13–4:6

# Concluding Note

The period of about four centuries between the Testaments is of immense importance for a right understanding of the New Testament. The Old Testament closed in the Medo-Persian period, and the New Testament opens in the Roman period, and between these is the great Grecian period. Between the Testaments the seat of world empire moved from the East to the West, from Asia to Europe. At this time arose Greek cities in Palestine, bearing Greek names, and the Hebrew scriptures were translated into Greek (70). Also in this period arose the sects of the Pharisees, the Sadducees, and the Essenes, and the Sanhedrin came into existence. In Malachi's time the Temple of Zerubbabel was standing, but in Matthew's time, the Temple of Herod. Synagogues also arose in this period, which are so prominent in the New Testament. To this time also we are indebted for the fourteen books of the Apocrypha, some of which, such as the two Maccabees, the Wisdom of Solomon, and Ecclesiasticus, are of great literary and historical importance. It was also in this period that the doctrine of immortality was taught by Plato. While these apocryphal writings are not regarded as holy Scripture, they must not be neglected by the Bible student. Though we have no inspired writings of this period, God was not inactive, and the fulfilment of His redeeming purpose was progressing towards 'the fulness of the time', when Christ would appear.